WELSH IN THE OLD WEST

By

Lorin Morgan-Richards

Foreword by Jude Johnson

This book is dedicated to Berlin

Revised 2024
A Raven Above Press
Copyright 2015
Studio City, CA
www.aravenabovepress.com

ISBN: 978-0-9830020-9-3

Other related titles from A Raven Above Press:

Me'ma and the Great Mountain
By Lorin Morgan-Richards

The Goodbye Family and the Great Mountain
By Lorin Morgan-Richards

The Goodbye Family series collection of panel comic books

www.lorinrichards.com

INDEX

Foreword	5
Author's Introduction	7
Welsh Cattle Drovers	9
Daniel Boone	11
Oliver Evans	12
John Rice Jones	15
John Thomas Evans	16
Meriwether Lewis	17
William Sherley Williams	20
Evan Jones	22
James "Jim" Bowie	23
John Plumbe Jr.	26
Colonel Cadwallader Jones	28
William Fargo	31
Dan Jones	33
Alexander Hamilton Swan	36
Morgan Jones	38
Colonel John Hunt Morgan	40
Robert Vaughn	43
Elias Morris	44
Annie Ellis	46
Jessie James	49
Frank James	56
Henry Clay Vaughn	57
Jesse Evans	61
John Reynolds Hughes	64
Major William H. Llewellyn	67
John T. Morris	70
William R. "Jake" Owen	73
John Wightman (Frank Clifford)	74
David Robert Evans	77
Robert Mills (Owen Roscomyl)	78
John Perrett	80
Willa Cather	82
Harvey Logan	84
Old West ghost towns that have Welsh origins	88

Foreword

Jude Johnson, author, Cactus Cymry—Influential Welsh in the Southern Arizona Territory

When in the Course of human events, it becomes necessary for one people to dissolve the political bands which have connected them with another, and to assume among the powers of the earth...

Oh wait, wrong document. Then again, the Declaration of Independence *was* conceived, co-written, and presented to the Continental Congress by two prominent men of Welsh heritage, John Adams and Thomas Jefferson. According to the Welsh Society of Philadelphia (begun in 1729, and thus the oldest ethnic society of its kind in the US), sixteen signers of the Declaration were of direct Welsh descent, including Wales-born Francis Lewis (of Llandaff, Glamorganshire). Another fifteen had at least some Welsh blood, including John and Samuel Adams. One could conceivably argue that the conquest and continual oppression of Wales by England since the late thirteenth century fermented over the generations to finally boil into the American Revolution. One needs only to research Parliament's particular persecution of Sam Adams' father and the hardship it caused to see the seeds of resentment and revenge bloom in Samuel Adams' radical Sons of Liberty.

We hold these truths to be self-evident, that all men are created equal, that they are endowed by their Creator with certain unalienable Rights: that among these are Life, Liberty and the pursuit of Happiness.

Beleaguered at home by heavy-handed English rule, a collapsed economy, and imminent starvation at the end of the Napoleonic Wars, a large number of Welsh flocked to America in the early nineteenth century. Many chose to proudly declare and celebrate their heritage, joining large Welsh communities in Pennsylvania, Ohio, and Tennessee

Then there was the siren call of The American West: home on the range, purple mountain majesty, and Manifest Destiny. Wide open spaces, few to no rules, it exuded a magnetism to pursue happiness like nowhere else.

Many Welshmen (*Cymry,* in their language) decided to disappear in the West via assimilation, as was the case for the Welsh in the Arizona

Territory. Arizona is the only state that never had a concentrated Welsh community or a settlement that built a specific Welsh chapel. Many usual sources of documentation, such as baptismal certificates or chapel family rosters, therefore didn't exist in Territorial papers.

In this book, you'll find a varied collection of biographies of Welsh in The West. Some names you will recognize, such as Daniel Boone and Meriwether Lewis. According to several sources, Thomas Jefferson read, spoke, and wrote Welsh based on his correspondence with Meriwether Lewis detailing the Northwest Passage across America.

Da iawn! Who needed to cypher a code when one could write in *Cymraeg*?

But the lesser-known Welshmen hold a fascination as well. Not all fit the stereotype of the Welsh miner, for they were photographers, financiers, religious fanatics, and outlaws. In this book you'll glimpse a wide spectrum of folks who shaped The West, leaving an indelible Welsh mark on generations to come, still striving in that pursuit of happiness.

Author's Introduction

Pioneers began crossing over into New Spain (Louisiana Territory) in hopes of building settlements west of the Mississippi River. Native American cultures had already been living on these lands prior to it becoming a territory, creating even more hardship, conflict and diminished resources for their people. In 1797, one of the first pioneers to settle in this region was a Welshman named John Rice Jones, who was acting as an interpreter for Moses Austin in the business of lead mines. Soon after, Daniel Boone, of Welsh ancestry, at sixty-five years old, left Kentucky looking for more "more elbow room".

In the early years of American expansionism: inventors, journeymen, notorious outlaws, and everyday people impacted the natural course of what is today considered the Old West. Some were looking to make a name for themselves, others looked to prosper from it, while many were just trying to survive. This unique collection of biographical stories offers a glimpse into their lives as Welsh emigrants and descendants and their importance during American expansionism. The biographies are shared in a chronological time line that corresponds to major events around them.

In curating the artwork I believed it was important to establish a contemporary bridge to paint the past. Welsh in the Old West is illustrated by published artists residing in both the United States and Wales and in various fields from pen and ink to acrylic, photography, modeling, collage and oil. There is quite a diversity in the depictions equal to those biographies in this book.

I hope you enjoy this collection as much as I had in making it.

The following are suggested for further reading about Welsh emigrants and descendants in the Old West: Jude Johnson's *Cactus Cymry— Influential Welsh in the Southern Arizona Territory,* Dafydd Meirion's *Welsh Cowboys and Outlaws, and* Eirug Davies' *Y Cymry ac Aur Colorado.*

Haiptrw Ho!
Lorin Morgan-Richards

Welsh Cattle Drovers

It is important to begin our collection with the Welsh cattle drovers (porthmyn), who were the precursor of many cowboys covered in this book. These drovers were cattlemen in Wales and most prolific between the 17th and 19th centuries, until the introduction of the railroad. Drovers traveled great length usually on foot, but sometimes on horseback, driving 200 plus cattle from feed to market. Often drovers would go several weeks at about 200 miles to feed, and then another equal distance to get them to market in London, Manchester or Birmingham. The assistance of dogs was a necessity on the trail, for their natural homing device to ensure they led the drovers back home.

Roads that were cut specifically for and by drovers have in some cases dated back to early Roman times. While other drover trails have become modernized, and these can be identified by their sudden turns that the drover would have found helpful against wind currents and inclement weather.

Professor Moore-Colyer of the University of Wales, Aberystwyth, an expert on drovers speaks of their character, "the drovers were a pretty tough lot. The first reactions of people in the villages they passed through was to lock up their wives, daughters and animals." "Haiptrw Ho! Haiptrw Ho! And a droving I shall go!", was the call of the drovers, meaning get out of their way as they would venture through. While farmers tended to be in favor of the drovers and their generous dealings, a letter to Sir Robert Williams, the Seventh Viscount Bulkeley's half brother, tells a different story:

"I am really very sorry to find that a number of your tenants have been defrauded of a considerable sum of money for cattle by a set of men, who called themselves 'Drovers'. but who by the way are in general complete swindlers."

The drovers endured a life of hardship, traveling great lengths for a mere night or two of reverly. To some they were seen as outcasts whom made their own rules, but to those who relied on their services, they were praised for their work.

The Welsh in America

John Thomas Evans, artist: Anna Hughes (page 16)

Artist: Michele Witchipoo

Daniel Boone

Daniel Boone was born on November 2, 1734 (O.S. October 22) in Reading, Pennsylvania. Boone's maternal grandfather Edward Morgan originated in Gwynedd, North Wales. Boone was brought up in a large family of Quakers and was responsible for a number of chores on their farm. He was an adapt hunter in his youth and developed a skill for sharpshooting. What he caught and was able to trade provided his family necessities through difficult times. Boone's first adventures outside the farm included participating in the French and Indian War, where he drove supply wagons.

In later life, Boone headed west, and it is his role in helping open the Cumberland Gap that historians argue is his most memorable accomplishment. The westward route passed through the Appalachian Mountains and in 1767 his Wilderness Road was the foremost route to travel. Boone writes of his trek in 1769:

We proceeded successfully, and after a long and fatiguing journey through a mountainous wilderness, in a westward direction, on the seventh day of June following we found ourselves on Red-River, where John Finley had formerly been trading with the Indians, and, from the top of an eminence, saw with pleasure the beautiful level of Kentucky. We found everywhere abundance of wild beasts of all sorts, through this vast forest. The buffalo were more frequent than I have seen cattle in the settlements, browzing on the leaves of the cane, or cropping the herbage on those extensive plains, fearless, because ignorant, of the violence of man. Sometimes we saw hundreds in a drove, and the numbers about the salt springs were amazing.

Following expeditions included constructing a fort, Boonesborough, in what is now Kentucky. Boone lived in the woods with his wife and family of 10 children outside colonial settlements. During a time of war and conquest, his family befell several attacks and captures by hostile parties of Native Americans. In one incident, he lost his son.

Boone was an officer in the American Revolution for the Virginia militia and later served as state legislature for several terms. Boone died on September 26, 1820 and was laid to rest in Kentucky, where his adventures as a frontiersman live on.

Oliver Evans

Evans was born on September 13, 1755 in Newport, Delaware, to a family of Welsh settlers.

In his teens, Evans was fascinated by mathematics and mechanics and apprenticed a wheelwright and wagonmaker. One day he observed a trick originally done by a blacksmith's boy who used steam to prank his father. The boy poured water in a gun barrel and rammed wadding down it. He then set the butt end of the gun in his father's smithing fire. The steam ejected the wadding with a bang as loud as gunpowder. This simple idea led Evans to investigate ways to harness steam for propulsion.

Before the age of 29, Evans solved several industrial problems from mechanical sheering to an automated mill in Philadelphia. The only labor involved was starting the inventions in motion. In the case of the mill, it was powered by waterwheels, and rough grain went in from one end through a system of conveyors and chutes to mill and refine it until it produced a fine flour when it was finished.

Evans third invention was the high-pressured steam engine, patent protected at the state level in 1787 and in 1790 at the U.S. Patent Office. His vision was two-fold, a stationary engine that could be used in factories and another for travel over land and water. Evans engineered the steam engine's beam so that the cylinder and the crankshaft were on the same side, reducing the beam's weight, and making road transportation possible. Evans was denied its use as riding by horse was the major mode of travel and authorities feared it might frighten them. The engines however found a place within the workplace, including sowing grain, driving sawmills, boring machines, and powering a dredge to remove dirt.

In 1805, the first steam-engine vehicle to be used on roads in the United States was Evan's scow, called the Orukter Amphibolos, or Amphibious Digger. It measured 30 feet long by 12 feet wide and it utilized a chain of buckets similar to his automatic flour mill.

Building on his success Evans developed his Mars Iron Works that began production in 1806 for more than 100 steam engines with

Artist: Nichola Hope

various uses from processing cotton, tobacco, to paper. Evans even proposed to build a powerful steamship with a large gun for the Navy during the War of 1812. But the proposal was turned down. It took 50 years before something similar would be created.

Evans completed in 1817 a 24-horsepower high-pressure engine for waterworks, but died shortly after when a fire engulfed his Mars Iron Works, including unknown patterns and molds. Evans died on April 15, 1819.

Evans was a major contributor to the fields of automation, materials handling and steam power. Evans was prolific and influential as an inventor; designing the first high-pressured steam engine and automobile in the United States, and the first fully automated industrial process to name a few. Evans books have been in production for generations including: *Young Mill-Wright and Miller's Guide* (1792) and in *The Abortion of the Young Steam Engineer's Guide* (1805), which in the latter should be noted for its plea for government subsidization of technological advances.

John Rice Jones

John Rice Jones was born in Mallwyd, Wales on February 10 (or 11), 1759. After attending Oxford University he practiced law in London. He immigrated to the United States in 1784 and for a time lived in Philadelphia. By 1785 Jones had an itch to head west and landed in Vincennes, present-day Indiana. Here, he joined a militia led by George Rogers Clark to defend the area against Wabash Indian retaliations for seizing their land.

Nearing the end of the uprising, Jones moved again to Kaskaskia, on the east bank of the Mississippi River. In 1789 Jones scouted for the militia providing valuable insight into the Spanish plans to remove the settlements on the American side of the river. Jones ability to speak French, English, and Spanish made him well known and even more persuasive as an attorney. According to Lt. Gov. Zenon Trudeau the "caustic character of the lawyer Jones whom you have seen, aside from his wrangling's, has a talent destined to trouble us." In 1797, Jones was invited to serve as an interpreter for Moses Austin during his visit to the Upper Louisiana's lead mines. Austin seeking the benefit of Jones' relationship drew in partnership with him at Mine a Breton, west of Ste. Genevieve.

In 1801, Jones was asked back to Vincennes where he was appointed Indiana Territory's first attorney general by Governor William Henry Harrison. By 1805 Jones was serving as a member of the territory's Legislative Council but was unable to win a Congressional later for his unpopular view of proslavery.

After 1810 Jones resettled at Mine a Breton continuing his partnership with Moses Austin. Together they were able to establish the town of Potosi but could not see eye to eye on other affairs and dissolved their joint interests. Jones died on February 1, 1824, before finishing his first term on the Missouri Supreme Court.

John Thomas Evans

John Thomas Evans was born into a Methodist family on April of 1770 in the village of Waunfawr, Gwynedd, Wales. Evans, was a patriotic student and fascinated with history. While attending university in London, Evans joined a Welsh group looking to promote Wales as a cultural unique entity from the British Isles. One of those he befriended was the influential poet Iolo Morganwg who related a translation of the Madoc legend suggested Madoc discovered America and that there may exist "Welsh Indians". According to legend, Madoc left Wales in 1170 upon the death of his father King Owain of Gwynedd. His journey west and apparent finding of land was retold upon his return. He is said to have sailed back with a boat of families looking to settle the new world.

Evans was asked by Morganwg to travel with him to America to seek out this lost tribe. However, Morganwg's plans fell through and left Evans to go alone. In October of 1792 Evans arrived in Baltimore and by the spring of the following year, made his way to St. Louis into the Spanish Territory of Louisiana. Evans was imprisoned under the suspicion of being a British spy.

In 1795, Evans convinced his captures to back an exploration up the Missouri River and find a route to the Pacific Ocean in the name of the Spanish crown.

Evans visited the Mandans, Hidatsu and Arikara between 1796 and 1797 but did not find sufficient evidence for "Welsh Indians". His failure was not completely fruitless as the detailed maps he produced became vital for future expeditions in present day North and South Dakota. Notably, Meriwether Lewis and William Clark used his maps up the Missouri River in 1804.

Evans died in New Orleans in May of 1799.

Meriwether Lewis

Meriwether Lewis was born on August 18, 1774 in Albemarle County, Virginia. His ancestry in Wales goes back to one Robert Lewis, born in Brecon around 1574, and whose son, also named Robert, emigrated to America in 1635.

Lewis's father, Lt. William Lewis, died of phenomena when Meriwether was six. Shortly after, his mother and stepfather moved the family to the Broad River Valley in Georgia, an area known to be Cherokee territory. Lewis became adept at hunting and living as a woodsman, and at a very early age he was providing for his family and protecting them.

By 1787, Lewis was sent back to Virginia for private tutoring. He graduated in 1793 from Liberty Hall (present day Washington and Lee University). In the same year, he joined the Virginia militia during the Whisky Rebellion and further upheld military service going through the ranks of Captain in the US Army where he met a seasoned William Clark in 1801.

On April 1, 1801 Lewis was appointed an aide to President Thomas Jefferson, an old acquaintance of the Virginia society. Jefferson saw potential in Lewis, and with the promise for expansion, the immediate threat of European land claims and necessity to trade with Native American cultures along the Missouri River (something the French and Spanish had gained financially from). Jefferson elected Lewis to lead an expedition to explore the territory of the Louisiana Purchase (post-New Spain), declare sovereignty over the Indigenous people, and lay claim to the Pacific Northwest and Oregon Country for the United States. Approved by Congress in January of 1803, Lewis was left with the task of recruiting his team which included William Clark and a slave named York. The exploration began May 14, 1804.

On October 10, 1804, Lewis wrote in his journal:

The weather was this day fine, and as we were desirous of assembling the whole nation at once, we despatched Mr. Gravelines, who with Mr. Tabeau another French trader had breakfasted with us, to invite the

Artist: Rochelle Rosenkild

chiefs of the two upper villages to a conference. They all assembled at one o'clock, and after the usual ceremonies we addressed them in the same way in which we had already spoken to the Ottoes and Sioux: we then made or acknowledged three chiefs, one for each of the three villages; giving to each a flag, a medal, a red coat, a cocked hat and feather, also some goods, paint and tobacco, which they divided among themselves: after this the airgun was exhibited, very much to their astonishment, nor were they less surprised at the colour and manner of York. On our side we were equally gratified at discovering that these Ricaras made use of no spirituous liquors of any kind, the example of the traders who bring it to them so far from tempting having in fact disgusted them. Supposing that it was as agreeable to them as to the other Indians, we had at first offered them whiskey; but they refused it with this sensible remark, that they were surprised that their father should present to them a liquor which would make them fools. On another occasion they observed to Mr. Tabeau, that no man could be their friend who tried to lead them into such follies.

In November of 1804, Sacajawea, who acted as a Shoshone interpreter, and her French husband Toussaint Charbonneau joined the commissioned unit (Corps of Discovery). Sacajawea gave birth to a child (Jean Baptiste on February 11, 1805) on the journey, and would eventually met her own birth family that she had been kidnapped from on a raid by the Hidatsas. William Clark wrote of the importance of Sacajawea:

"The wife of Shabono our interpreter we find reconciles all the Indians, as to our friendly intentions a woman with a party of men is a token of peace".

In 1806, Lewis was appointed Governor of Upper Louisiana by President Thomas Jefferson. On September 3, 1809, Lewis left for Washington, D.C., to resolve an impending debt he had for denied payments of drafts against the War Department. Lewis took with him several journals for publishing. He rerouted his travels, instead taking the Natchez Trace, or old pioneer road between Natchez and Nashville. Lewis was said to have been in a depressed state on the journey and had already written his will. On October 10th of that year, Lewis checked in at Grinder's Stand Inn, southwest of Nashville and died mysteriously in the early morning hours of the 11th from several gunshot wounds.

William Sherley "Old Bill" Williams

William Sherley Williams was born January 3, 1787 in Western North Carolina near present day Polk County. Williams was of strong Welsh descent from both sides of his family, closest of which was his grandfather John Williams who was born in Wales and emigrated to America.

Williams relocated with his family in 1794 to St. Louis, where the family continued farming. By the age of seventeen, following an education, Williams took up Baptist ministry on the frontier. Around 1813, he lived with the Osage and married an Osage woman, having two daughters. Williams left the ministry in his mid-twenties and refocused on trapping, one of the chief exports of St. Louis at the time.

Williams was hired on several occasions for his trusted guidance and skill at surviving in what was deemed unexplored areas. Between 1825 and 1826 Williams was part of a surveying team that tracked a sizeable portion of the Santa Fe Trail. Williams was friendly with several Native American cultures and could speak their languages. In his experience he had crossed a wide area of exploration west of Missouri. From 1833–34 he was a member of a California expedition and in 1841 and 1843 he entered areas of the Northwest and New Mexico. Notably, in 1848 he was a guide for an expedition led by John Charles Fremont through the Colorado mountains which proved disastrous due to poor leadership and torrential snowstorms. Williams was blamed and several weeks after he tried to return to salvage some of the lost equipment.

On March 14, 1849, Williams and his party, unknowing that a village of Utes had been recently decimated by soldiers, sat quietly at a campfire on the upper Rio Grande in southern Colorado. The party was met by Utes who they engaged in a friendly manner. But two of the Utes in revenge, came up from behind and fired shots at Williams and a Dr. Kern, striking them dead.

Artist: Kimberly Wlassak

Evan Jones

Evan Jones was born in Brecknockshire, Wales on May 14, 1788. He spoke both Welsh and English, and at the age of fifteen apprenticed as a linen-draper. His parents expected him to finish his apprenticeship and earn a living as a tradesman, but having less interest in the field, and having fallen in love with his co-worker, Elizabeth Lanigan, the two moved to London and married on December 31, 1810. They became Methodists and Jones took to tutoring and teaching. Unfortunately this career was short lived and Jones went back to work as a draper, opening a shop near Ludgate Hill in London. While raising a small family, Jones struggled in the business and after 13 years he emigrated with his family to America in 1821.

The Jones family settled in the Welsh community of Berwyn, near Philadelphia. Jones joined the Great Valley Baptist Church and during the summer of 1821, Evan Jones saw an ad at the church for volunteers to become missionaries among the Cherokee. His entire family left to volunteer and by September they arrived in North Carolina, where he taught and preached at the Valley Town Baptist Mission. Jones became close with some the Cherokee, including pupils Jesse Bushyhead and future chief Lewis Downing. With the help of his pupils, especially Bushyhead, Jones learned to speak and write the Cherokee language, and volunteered to mediate between their leaders and the US Government. Evans and Bushyhead were with the Cherokees during the forced removal to Indian Territory in present day Oklahoma.

Life was not kind to Jones, having lost his first wife on February 5, 1831 and most of his children during his mission work. The surviving son, John Buttrick Jones, continued his work and also became an advocate for the Cherokee. Evan Jones died August 18, 1872 in Tahlequah, Cherokee Nation, Oklahoma.

James "Jim" Bowie

James Bowie was born in Logan County (present day Simpson County), Kentucky around April 10, 1796 to parents Reason (Rezin) Bowie of Scottish descent, and Elve Ap-Catesby Jones, the daughter of a Welsh immigrant.

Bowie's early years were on the family farm where they also owned a gristmill and had slaves. By February of 1800 the family moved to Madrid, present day Missouri. In the following year, Reason with his brothers swore allegiance to Spain at Rapides, Louisiana to settle in what is now Catahoula Parish. Bowie was raised here and by 1809 the entire clan resettled in Atakapa country where Reason bought 640 acres to develop a plantation.

As a teenager Bowie worked in the parishes of Avoyelles and Rapides, transporting lumber. He was active in hunting and fishing and known to even ride wild horses and alligators and was an experienced bear trapper. Bowie was handsome with high cheek bones, a fair complexion and green eyes but also had a less than appealing temper when riled.

When the War of 1812 broke out, Bowie and his brother Rezin Jr. joined the Second Division which was compiled of rough hardy men of the area. At the turn of 1815, they were deployed to Andrew Jackson march on New Orleans but the war ended before they saw action.

Following the war, Bowie and his brother took to trading slaves with a pirate named Jean Laffite, who was stealing slave ships in the Caribbean and Gulf of Mexico. It was a large criminal operation Bowie entered into, profiting $65,000 by the time he left the business. The two also engaged in land speculation and worked hard at keeping good relations with wealthy land owners, while making enemies with those who opposed him.

In 1826, while in Alexandra, Bowie was attacked by Norris Wright, but the bullet missed its mark. Ever after, Bowie carried a large butcher-like hunting knife, a present from his brother. The notorious weapon was first used near Natchez on September 19, 1827 when a duel led into an all out brawl (the Sandbar Fight) involving Bowie and Wright. Shots were fired, and Bowie was struck in the lower chest. According to an eye witness Bowie "drew his butcher knife which he usually wears" and chased Wright. Bowie was again shot and stabbed several times. Wright lurching over him, Bowie fatally plunged the knife into Wright's breast and lifted himself to slash his other attackers. The fight ended, and reports surged afterwards of Bowie's resilience and superior blade that many men were asked to craft in its likeness, the Bowie Knife.

Bowie had plans to marry Cecelia Wells in 1829, but she died two weeks before their wedding. Bowie continued wheeling and dealing in landholdings making him substantial money for the time. Bowie's brother John shares his feelings of the Sandbar Fight: After my brother (James) recovered from his wounds, he felt as though he had not been well used, or properly treated by some of his political friends, so he determined to leave the United States and go to Texas.

Bowie and a friend left for Mexican occupied Texas on January 1, 1830. In February he took an oath of allegiance to Mexico, and began his dealings of land purchasing and living as a gambler. Bowie took advantage of the Mexican law of 1828 that gave citizens over 4,000 acres in Texas for $100 to $250. Bowie wrangled Mexicans to buy and then sell him the land. This business dealing nonetheless bothered Stephen F. Austin, who had tracts of land in the Austin colony.

Bowie was now parading as a wealthy man in San Antonio where he befriended the Veramendi family, whom allowed him access to Mexican citizenship in 1830. He married Ursula de Veramendi on April 25, 1831, and promised the family he would establish wool and cotton mills in Coahuila for their support. Bowie would not sit still for long and after the honeymoon in New Orleans and Natchez, he found himself adventuring in Indian Territory. He was now considered a "colonel" of citizen rangers and animosity grew between the Anglo citizens and the government.

In July, Mexican Commander José de las Piedras, told the Anglo citizens to surrender their arms and Bowie left for Nacogdoches with James W. Bullock and a 300 strong militia. Piedras was sieged and fled. Bowie and his men took Nacogdoches on March 9, 1833. This was the first major battle in a string to come.

In September Bowie lost his wife, a child (at least one), and her parents to cholera in the city of Monclova. Bowie who befell yellow fever in Natchez was unaware of his loss. He wrote his will on October 31.

Between 1834 and 1835 Mexican laws opened a wide range of land speculations in Texas. Bowie was asked to serve as commissioner of the Coahuilla-Texas government's settlement and 400-league parcel for a frontier defense. In May, Santa Anna looked to arrest any Texan doing business in Monclova. Bowie fled and on June 22 wrote Mexico and Texas ties were severed. War was eminent.

On February 2, 1836, Bowie was stationed in Bexar at the Alamo Mission and urged Governor Smith for supplies and men. Lieutenant Travis rode in with thirty at first, then an additional twelve volunteers with David Crockett, all together they numbered 150. Bowie was elected in command, and disgraced Travis who initially was in charge with a drunken event. Travis left with his men but soon returned to negotiate with Bowie how the command would be split.

On February 23 they learned a force of 1,500 Mexican cavalrymen were in route. By this time, Bowie had weaken from either a type of pneumonia or tuberculosis and would spend his last days confined to a cot, redirecting his volunteers to listen to Travis.

The Mexican force attacked just before dawn on March 6, 1836 killing all the defenders of the Alamo. Santa Anna wanted to see the corpse of Bowie who was found on his cot shot several times in the head.

John Plumbe Jr.

John Plumbe Jr. was born on July 13, 1809 in the village of Castle Caereinion, Powys, Wales. John Plumbe and Frances Margaretta Atherton emigrated to Philipsburg, Pennsylvania in 1821.

Around 1827, Plumbe acted as apprentice civil engineer for a rail system across the Allegheny Mountains. Plumbe went on to work on the first interstate railroad in Virginia and North Carolina five years later. He left with the Plumbe family to Dubuque, Wisconsin Territory (present day Iowa) in 1836 where they spent the rest of their days. He developed real estate along the Mississippi River and drafted a plan for Congress to build the first segment of the transcontinental railroad, running from Lake Michigan to western Iowa. Sometime in March of 1840, Plumbe was in Boston promoting the idea of his railroad expansion and came upon the daguerreian process in photography. Short on funds and waiting to receive a commission from Congress to survey the transcontinental route, Plumbe took to the new interest and began advertising himself as a "Professor of Photography" by May of 1841. Interestingly, photography was such a strange phenomenon to most that his first establishment had to share a bill with a lady magician, a phrenologist, and a tattooed man. By the summer, Plumbe opened several new galleries in Exeter, New Hampshire, Salem, Mass, and Dubuque, Iowa Territory, and Philadelphia.

Plumbe was assigned a patent in 1842 for coloring daguerreotypes, and continued opening galleries along the east coast. A total of 25 galleries were counted by 1845 reaching into the Midwest. His concept of "operating" these galleries was a pioneering approach at franchising and brand- -name recognition. All the photographs from these various location were stamped "Plumbe".

All was not fruitful however, in 1847, Plumbe went into bankruptcy citing over competition, unscrupulous operators, and declining business. All of Plumbe's galleries were sold or transferred to the operators by late 1850.

Plumbe left for California in the spring of 1849 to pursue his original dream of a transcontinental railroad. In the mid-1850s, he had a severe malaria attack, and returned to Dubuque to live with his brother.

Stricken with ill health, the panic of 1857 left him further in debt. On May 29, 1857 he took his own life by slitting his throat.

Plumbe would be remembered as an early advocate of a transcontinental railroad and America's first nationally known professional photographer.

Colonel Cadwallader Jones

Colonel Cadwallader Jones was born 1813 in Hillsboro, Orange County, North Carolina. Jones was a descendant of Richard Jones of Wales, whose family left the homeland to Virginia in the late 1600's. Jones was born of Col. Cadwallader Jones II from "Monte Cailoux" near Petersburg, VA and wife Rebecca Edwards Long of North Carolina.

Jones went to school in Hillsboro, North Carolina at W. A. Bingham, and graduated at the University of North Carolina at the age of nineteen. He began studying law and entered a practice in Raleigh in 1834. After a short time he left for Hillsboro to work as an attorney. On January 5, 1836, he married Annie Isabella Iredell, a high standing young woman who was the eldest daughter of North Carolina Gov. James Iredell, Jr..

Jones work and family position led him to represent Orange Co, North Carolina in the General Assembly of 1840 and 1842. He was also elected and served as solicitor of the 4th Judicial circuit until 1856. By 1857, he removed his growing family to South Carolina to start a plantation.

With the oncoming Civil War, Jones raised a company in 1861 for the Confederate States Army and led as their Captain. When Gregg's Brigade launched the 12th South Carolina Infantry Regiment, Jones was promoted to Major and then Lieutenant Colonel. On October 1, 1862 he gave the following report.

SIR: I have the honor to submit detailed reports of the part taken by the Twelfth Regiment South Carolina Volunteers in the battles of Manassas, August 29 and 30; of Ox Hill, September 1; of Harper's Ferry, September 15; Sharpsburg, September 17, and Shepherdstown, September 20:

This duty devolves on me in consequence of the death of Colonel Dixon Barnes, late commander of this regiment. He fell mortally wounded at the battle of Sharpsburg in the third and last charge of his regiment, and just as the tide of battle had turned decisively in his favor. He was then, as always, in the midst of his command. Justice to our lamented colonel authorizes me to say a more gallant officer has

Artist: Carys Evans

not fallen during the war. Distinguished alike for dashing courage in battle, for a most amiable and gentlemanly bravery in social life, and for strict military discipline everywhere, we feel that his loss is irreparable to his regiment, which he so much honored by his gallantry, and which in turn has honored him by its distinguished bravery whenever brought in the face of the foe. He lingered of his wounds, being shot in both knees, until September 27, on which day he departed this life at Charlestown, Virginia.

Jones also a victim of ill health was forced to resign in late September 1862. Jones returned to South Carolina and was elected as senator from York. In 1865 he was a delegate to the constitutional convention. Jones died on December 1, 1899 in Columbia, Richland County, South Carolina.

William Fargo

William Fargo was born on May 20, 1818 in Pompey, New York. His ancestor Moses Fargo left Wales in 1668 aboard the "Armenia," arriving in present day Norwich, Connecticut. It is possible that his Welsh ancestral origin is in a place called Sidney as the birthplace of Jacent Fargo, and historical records do show a place called Sidney, Monmouthshire, Wales. However the exact location still remains a mystery.

At the age of 13, he worked for a contractor delivering mail over a 30-mile circuit and after took several odd jobs. He married in 1840 to Anna H. Williams, by whom they had three children.

In the following years, Fargo refocused his career as a messenger for an express operation from Albany to Buffalo. Building on his success and negotiating relations with Henry Wells in 1843 as an agent for Livingston, Wells, and Pomeroy's Express. Afterwards he helped found Wells & Company, the first express service west of Buffalo. Fargo also became the founder of the American Express Company.

In 1852, Fargo went into partnership with Henry Wells and created Wells, Fargo, & Company to provide service to gold mining towns of California. American Express and Wells Fargo worked together to become the fastest transportation of goods and communication between points on the east and west coasts.

The financial panic in 1855 sunk many of their competitors, while Wells Fargo continued to grow and by 1857, with American Express founded the Overland Mail, the first transcontinental stagecoach line.

The railroad in 1869 could have stifled business transactions but with another merger of the Pacific Express Company on the new transcontinental railroad in the west, and similarly with American Express in the east they were again strategically sound.

During the Civil War, Fargo was mayor of Buffalo between 1862 and 1866, and believed against secession. He supported Union troops with a stipend of his salary for anyone he employed that was drafted.

Artist: Sarah Hope

Later in life, he acted as director of both the Northern Pacific Railroads and New York Central. Upon Wells retirement in 1868, Fargo took over presidency of the American Express Company, and held this until his death on August 3, 1881.

James Fargo, brother of William, founded the Merchants Dispatch Transportation Company, and succeeded as President of American Express. James, having difficulty on a European trip in cashing checks, saw the necessity of a new product he introduced in 1891 in the form of travelers checks.

Dan Jones

Dan Jones was born on August 4, 1810 in Halkin, North Wales. The sixth of eight children of Thomas and Ruth Jones who were devote Methodists. Dan Jones became a mariner at the age of sixteen, traveling international waters. On January 3, 1837 he married Jane Melling of Denbigh and the two emigrated to St. Louis, Missouri in 1841. Here he worked as captain of steamers along the Mississippi River.

Jones had become influenced by the writings of the Church of the Latter Day Saints and met Prophet Joseph Smith on April 12, 1843 when he was aboard his steamer at Nauvoo, Illinois a refuge for the Mormons. The two became friendly and it was not long before Jones became his closest admirer.

In June of 1844, after the destruction of a Mormon paper, Non-Mormons demanded the arrest of Smith criticizing his leadership and the religious practice of polygamy. Acting in fear, Smith armed several of his converts and declared martial law. In Carthage, Illinois, a state militia led by Governor Thomas Ford asked for Smith's surrender. Smith escaped across the Mississippi River, but returned and surrendered. Smith would stand trial for treason and those involved including Jones were imprisoned in Carthage.

On the night before the 27th, Smith perhaps seeing his own fate asked Jones if he was afraid to die. Jones responded, "Has that time come think you? Engaged in such a cause I do not think that death would have many terrors." It was then Smith instructed, "You will yet see Wales and fulfill the mission appointed you ere you die." Smith gave a letter to Jones who was able to leave on account of requesting a lawyer. The jail was overtaken by a mob, bursting through the door, shooting and killing Hyrum Smith, Joseph's older brother. Joseph who hid a small pepper box pistol fired back and made his way for the window. Smith jumped out and was shot dead. Jones was apparently shot at when he rode away on his horse but was able to evade the bullets.

In the following months Jones prepared and left for Wales. It would be the first of several missions. His wife Jane accompanied his first voyage. Jones preferred to preach in Welsh and became involved with publishing Mormon literature. By January of 1849, after his first mission, there were nearly 4,000 Latter-day Saints in Wales.

At the end of the year, while in Salt Lake City, Jones married a second plural wife, Elizabeth Jones Lewis and on February 18, 1857, he would marry a third, Mary Matilda LaTrielle. The Jones family would resettle in Provo, Utah Territory, and on February 24, 1861, Jane died of tuberculosis. Jones died the following year on January 3rd, leaving six children, two by each wife.

Artist: Briana Lopez

Artist: Shelby Criswell

Alexander Hamilton Swan

Alexander Hamilton Swan, of Welsh descent, was born November 24, 1831 in Green County, Pennsylvania. Swan was notably the president of three successful cattle companies, and lived as a cattle rancher. Swan was described as being over six feet with a Duke of Wellington nose, and having gold teeth. He was an imposing figure to many, but also could charm just about anyone. In business and personal life, he was worshipped by those around him, whether at home in Cheyenne, Wyoming or on his trips like in Chicago where he was courted by bankers, commission men, and cattle breeders. At the height of success he was a million dollar man, but his fortunes were questionable.

Swan's career really began in 1873 when he and family members established one of the largest cattle companies in the West, the Swan Brothers Cattle Company. Swan managed the business, with 3,000 head of cattle in 1873 at the Two Bar Ranch on Chugwater Creek in southeastern Wyoming. By 1882 the company had a herd of 33,000 heads. In the following year he formed the Swan Land and Cattle Company and was able to sell it to Scottish investors for $2,550,825. While managing the company, Swan continued his growth of four more cattle companies. Swan was considered the first to introduce purebred Herefords from England to the United States.

Under Swan's watch, the Swan Land and Cattle Company expanded to a million acres and held over 110,000 heads of cattle. Swan was also in demand further east where he was brought in to build the Union Stockyards in Omaha, Nebraska.

Swan was also an active politician. In 1877, he served as a Republican to the council in the fifth Wyoming legislative assembly. While he ran for Congress in 1880, he was not successful and this seemed to be the beginning of trouble on the horizon. Between 1886 and 1887 his ranching ended due to a combination of overstocking, overgrazing, and a disastrous Wyoming winter that killed around 300,000 to 400,000 head of cattle. Swan went bankrupt and was accused by his detractors of poor management. He was sued by his own corporation and replaced by an aggressor. Swan left Cheyenne and died August 9, 1905 in Provo, Utah.

Artist: Sarah Hope

Morgan Jones

Morgan Jones was born near Tregynon, Montgomery County, Wales, on October 7, 1839 to Morgan Jones, Sr. and Mary Charles. At an early age Morgan Jr. was fascinated with trains and this catapulted his venture into transportation by the age of twenty. He worked as an apprentice for seven years with the Cambrian Railway Company before emigrating to the United States in 1866.

Jones skills were in high demand, leading him into a position with the Union Pacific Railroad as a foreman. In 1869, he managed a crew of construction workers who moved from Omaha to meet the Central Pacific from Sacramento to form the first transcontinental railroad in the United States.

Jones was also considered a local hero in Fort Worth when an unfinished Texas and Pacific line was just 16 miles short of Eagle Ford. An uncompleted track would compromise their charter and land subsidy. But Jones was hired and his project became "a patriotic crusade to bring the railroad home." Every Fort Worth citizen took part day and night to finish it. July 19, 1876 was declared a local holiday as Jones's line reached Fort Worth before the deadline.

By 1884, Jones was president of the Fort Worth and Denver City Railway Company and in 1906 he started the Abilene and Northern Railway. Jones moved to Abilene in 1908 and continued railroad expansion finishing the Abilene and Southern Railway.

Jones career spanned numerous railroad lines, laying more than 1,000 miles of track across Texas and the West. He held several successful investments and enterprises outside of transportation in industrial, farming, banking, lumber, and ranching. He was considered humble and shy and never allowed a photograph be taken or answer questions for a newspaper until he reached the age of eight three. Jones, a lifelong member of the Church of England, died on April 11, 1926 in Abilene.

Colonel John Hunt Morgan

John Hunt Morgan was born on June 1, 1825 in Huntsville, Alabama, and grew up on a farm outside Lexington, Kentucky. Morgan was a descendant of William Morgan from the village of Llandaff, Glamorganshire, Wales. William had two sons: James and Miles. These brothers emigrated from Wales in 1636 and their descendants carry a long history of achievement in the United States; including John Pierpoint Morgan through Miles, and James: John Hunt Morgan and his nephew Thomas Hunt Morgan who became a well-known geneticist winning a Nobel Peace Prize for his chromosome theory of inheritance.

John Hunt Morgan was expelled at Transylvania College in Lexington due to bad behavior and instead enlisted in the military with the 1st Kentucky Cavalry when the Mexican War broke out. He served under Zachary Taylor and was a leader at the Battle of Buena Vista. Returning to Kentucky Morgan started a hemp business and raised a militia called the 'Lexington Rifles' out of his own expense.

When succession was a concern, Morgan joined the new Southern Confederacy with his militia marching to Bowling Green to command under General Buckner. In April 1862, Morgan was appointed colonel and was involved in the Battle of Shiloh. His service led him to join the General Braxton Bragg's Army of Tennessee. Although he was officially in an attachment he took an informal approach. Morgan was known for quick daring raids and guerrilla type tactics.

Most notably on July 4, 1862, Morgan unleashed a destructive offensive through Kentucky, covering 1,000 miles over enemy lines, crippling trains, communication, taking supplies, arms and prisoners as he went. The raid was the talk of the nation and evoked fear of the Southern calvary man.

By October and November Morgan was leading raids that pushed 20,000 Union troops off the front lines to protect their interests. Morgan was being called the 'Thunderbolt of the Confederacy.'

In July of 1863, against the wishes of General Bragg, Morgan and 2,400 men crossed the Ohio and terrorized local defensives one thousand miles up the north bank of the river. This noted as 'Morgan's

Raid'. The rampage lasted three weeks from Tennessee, up through Kentucky, into Indiana and on to Columbiana, Ohio where he was said to have visited "cousins". This attack reached the farthest north of any Confederate troops during the war. He was finally stopped in Salineville, Ohio, where he was captured and sent to the Ohio State Penitentiary in Columbus. On November 26, 1863, Morgan escaped prison and found his way back home.

In April of the following year Morgan accepted the position of head of the Department of Southwestern Virginia.

Morgan also planned to attack Knoxville, Tennessee where there was pro-Union support but his life was cut short when on September 3rd he was ambushed and critically wounded by a Union private who once served under him. Morgan died on September 4, 1864.

Robert Vaughn

Robert Vaughn was born in Montgomeryshire, Wales on June 5, 1836. Vaughn was the third of six children and worked on the family farm. He left for London at the age of nineteen and engaged in flower gardening while learning the English language. He emigrated to New York City in 1858 where the clerk of court misspelled his name as "Vaughan", something he had to accept but annoyed him ever after.

In his early twenties Vaughn worked odd jobs in Rome, New York, Palmyra and Youngstown, Ohio and McLean County, Illinois. It was not until 1864 he tried his luck at placer mining and followed the rush to Last Chance Gulch in Montana. While mining near Helena he was also a butcher in Nelson Gulch. By 1869, Vaughn moved to Sun River Valley and became the first homesteader and private stockman of the area. Vaughn resettled in Great Falls and built up a commendable ranching operation. With his help the town of Vaughn was constructed just west of Great Falls, honoring him.

During the 1870s and 1880s Vaughn was in contact with the Blackfeet and other local Native Americans as his ranch sat in close proximity to the Blackfeet Reservation.

In 1886, Vaughn married Elizabeth Donahue of Toronto, Canada and had a daughter named Arvonia on January 1, 1888. The complicated birth left Vaughn a widower and sole support for the child. After the death of his wife, Vaughn sold the ranch and moved into Great Falls. Through investing, mining enterprises, and real estate the town grew with his dealings. Vaughn went through a second failed marriage continuing to raise his beloved daughter in a Block apartment of Great Falls.

In Vaughn's last years of life, he suffered from rheumatism and was forced to walk with a cane, but he was said to never have complained in public. He died on March 23, 1918, at his home with daughter Arvonia and son-in-law H.M. Sprague. His achievements as a businessman and civic leader empowered those around him and he was considered with such appreciation in Montana people nicknamed him "Uncle Bob." Today, in the Arvon Block of Great Falls, a restaurant called the Celtic Cowboy opened to honor Vaughn's legacy.

Artist: Geri E. Gallas

Elias Morris

Elias Morris was born on June 30, 1825 in Denbigh, Wales. He learned the skill of stone masonry at an early age from his father, who worked as a contractor on Conway Castle and the Conway Bridge. At the time the work was completed, he left for Liverpool to learn more of his trade. After a year, he returned to Wales, where he heard the Gospel of Jesus Christ. He converted to the religion and left for the United States. On May 23, 1852 he married his first wife, Mary Parry, who had also come from Wales. They traveled across the country to Independence Rock, Wyoming, where they inscribed in stone: ELIAS MORRIS and MARY P. MORRIS. Today, there are hundreds of names scratched in this rock, but as his was the most legible, he is considered the "first stone cutter of Utah."

The Morris family settled in Provo, where they heard plans of erecting the Salt Lake Temple. Morris who had been living poorly walked fifty miles to join the event. His efforts paid off as he given the honor of cutting and dressing part of its base. Enlivened by the possibilities, he moved his family to Salt Lake and was asked to work on the Temple Square. In Salt Lake City, he married his second wife Mary Lois Walker in May of 1856.

Morris started building homes and providing advice for the many brick or stone structures. He opened a brickyard, providing adobe, concrete pipe, concrete forms, and eventually fire brick. At one point "he was contracting for so much work it was hard to get time to complete an unfinished chimney on his own house. An unexpected storm in the middle of the night brought a wind so strong it blew down the partly-built chimney. Elias heard the crash and knew what it was. He turned to his wife and said, "Mary please get up, put on some of my old work clothes, get the lantern and the scrub bucket ... you are about to become a hod-carrier. I can't repair the chimney alone, so you must help me save my reputation." The chimney was rebuilt by morning.

Morris built several stone structures at Fort Douglas: the stone chapel, the post-office, to name a few. As years went by, Morris branched out to other ventures, including monument building. He is considered today one of the greatest builders of memorial markers of stone. Morris died on March 17, 1898 in Salt Lake City, Utah.

Annie Ellis

Annie Ellis was born in Dolgellau, Wales in 1847. She arrived in America with her older brother, but at the age of 13 she was deserted in Kansas City and left to fend for herself, until a charitable organization took her in.

Into adulthood, Ellis married David Rule, a carpenter who was 25 years older than her. Around 1870, they arrived in Abilene, Kansas, but they did not have much of a married life as Rule was traveling with the army. To make matters worse, her husband was murdered in Kansas City, in a heist for his money. Ellis was left with nothing. She decided to move to Ellsworth where she began working as a dancer in the rough business of saloons and dance halls. She recalled losing her friend Lizzie Palmer from a fight with another girl.

"There was some scratching and hair-pulling, and Lizzie received a scalp wound which became infected. She died from blood poisoning. A big crowd of cowboys was celebrating in town. When the news of Lizzie's death was announced, the men, always sentimental, voted to give her a big funeral."

Ellis left for Dodge City as the money went west, and each town seemed to spring up on the Kansas plains with its share of saloons, dance halls and hell raising. As a dance hall girl, it was her purpose to roister cowboys and gunmen to buy as much beer as possible. In her time, she met some of the most fabled rowdy characters of lawmen and outlaws. There was "Bat" Masterson, the famous sheriff and gun toter whose name was a chronicle of western exploits.

"He was like any of the rest of 'em," she said. *"He was standing behind a pile of street rails at the railroad station shootin' back and forth with a man named Peacock, who was just as well protected behind the old Log City Jail."* Ellis went on, *"They got a reputation for bein' brave from the way they showed off with a gun. They liked to poke a revolver in the face of an unarmed man and tell him to laugh, or shoot at some good fellow's feet and make him dance. But they never pulled a gun if they could help it, or if the other man was armed."*

In 1871 Annie became friends with James Butler "Wild Bill" Hickok who

Artist: Jo Mazelis

found work for her in an eating house. Eventually Annie saved enough money to open a lodging house of her own in Wichita.

She remarried after 1880 to a rich rancher named George Anderson. She was given money by her new husband to buy land from Bat Masterson and also to open another lodging house and restaurant on Second Avenue, Dodge City. There, many characters of the period came to stay and eat, including those she already knew and others like Luke Short and Bill Tilghman. Former deputy Tilghman had a falling out with Earp who was searching for him. It is said Tilghman borrowed one of Annie's dresses and was able to escape from the irate lawman.

According to the 1930 census, she was still living in Dodge City, and was listed as a widow. Ellis died of heart disease on April 9, 1931 having lived a long life from rags to riches.

Jesse James

Jesse James was born Sept. 5, 1847 to Robert James and Zerelda Cole Mimms on their farm near Kearney, Clay County, Missouri. His family line was originally from Pembrokeshire, Wales, and it was John James who emigrated in the early 1700s to Pennsylvania.

Jesse's father was a Baptist preacher who was swept up into gold fever and told his wife that he would call on the family when he would strike it rich. He left in 1850 for California and died once there of pneumonia.

Zerelda remarried a man named Simms but the relationship fell apart. She married a third time in 1855 to a Dr. Reuben Samuel. The couple had one child together named Archie Samuel. The boy was mentally handicapped. The farm had slaves, and when the Civil War began the family sided with the Confederacy. Evoking conviction in their cause, in 1863, Union soldiers raided and decimated their farm. Jesse was beaten near death by the troops trying to stop them.

At 17, Jesse gained his strength and joined his brother and cousin Cole Younger as guerrilla fighters under the command of William Clarke Quantrill. As the whole of Confederate forces were moved out of the area in early 1862, the guerrilla fighters continued to put pressure on the north's advance. In 1864, Jesse and his brother served under William "Bloody Bill" Anderson and later attacked Lawrence, Kansas.

One night after a day of battling Union troops, Jesse was sitting next to a campfire cleaning his weapons. Unfortunately, the pistol discharged and shot off the tip of his middle finger. He held back any emotion and said, "Well, if that ain't the dingus-dangest thing!" Thereafter he was nicknamed "Dingus" James.

By the end of the war, the James brothers galloped back to ruins of their farm. Since guerrillas were not seen by the North as part of the Confederacy they were treated as outlaws and rewards were stacked against them. In 1865, a false amnesty was offered for the guerrillas, and upon arriving in Lexington, Missouri, they were greeted instead with bullets. Jesse was knocked off his horse with a shot puncturing his lung. The guerrillas fled and Jesse managed to hide himself. Frank meanwhile was being chased by two of the Union cavalry and was able

Artist: Michele Witchipoo

to thwart their attack with several shots. The riders halted and returned to look for Jesse.

On the following day, Jesse was aided by a friendly farmer who found him near a creek bed. Jesse begged, "I don't want to die in a northern state." The man bandaged the boy and with the help of the stranger Jesse was sent back to his mother and stepfather in their new home of Nebraska. To Jesse's wishes he was sent south to Harlem, Missouri, where he stayed at a relative's house, John Mimms. Here he met and was nursed by a young Zerelda Mimms, his cousin, who had been given his mother's name. Over time the two fell in love and Zee, as he called her, was promised marriage when she was of age.

After recuperating, his mother and step-father revisited the family farm in Kearney where they rebuilt their lives. Jesse continued to have lung problems and carried a gun at all times.

The South was suffering a major blow from the war, and damage from the North left many starving and unable to recover. Jesse, Frank and Cole had seen the evils of war, and learned from it. On February 13, 1866, a bank robbery occurred in Liberty, Missouri. It was a gang of ten, with two going into the Clay County Savings Bank. Frank James and Cole Younger were identified. Frank went up to the cashiers and said calmly: "If you make any noise, you will be shot." The money was put into a wheat sack, and the first haul brought them $60,000. A student named George "Jolly" Wymore stood in the middle of the town square in amazement, and called out to one of the riders he recognized. The rider turned his saddle and shot him dead. A posse formed but was unable to find the robbers.

Following more heists to banks and trains, and more importantly evading the law, the gang was becoming somewhat legendary. The bandits were all known by their names but not their faces. They carried on their Northern revenge, excusing southerners from their dealings. "Are you a southerner?" Cole Younger would ask, taking a gold watch from a protesting man with a southern accent. "Yes, suh," he replied. Discussing his service as a Confederate, Cole stopped and yelled over the passenger car, "We don't rob southerners, especially Confederate soldiers." He repositioned his pistol in another's face, "but Yankees and detectives are not exempt."

On Jan. 31, 1874, at the age of twenty-seven Jesse and the gang made their way to Gadshill, a depot for the Iron Mountain Railroad. Jesse and Frank waived down the Little Rock Express. The train stopped and the gang jumped into its baggage car. Inside they opened the safe by shooting off its locks and stole $22,000. They carried up through the cars robbing the passengers as they went.

Jesse jumped off the train onto his horse and galloped up to the engine where Cole held the engineer. "Give her a toot, Cole!" Jesse exclaimed, watching Cole yank the whistle as he laughed like a child. Before they left, Jesse threw a rolled paper to the engineer. "Give this to the newspapers. We like to do things in style."

The paper read:

The Most Daring Train Robbery on Record! The southbound train of the Iron Mountain Railroad was stopped here this evening by five heavily armed men and robbed of ____ dollars. The robbers arrive at the station a few minutes before the arrival of the train and arrest the agent and put him under guard and then threw the train on the switch. The robbers were all large men, all being slightly under six feet. After robbing the train they started in a southerly direction. They were all mounted on handsome horses. ps. They are a hell of an excitement in this part of the country.

Bringing in such a wealthy hoard, the gang settled down for a year. On April 23, 1874 Jesse married Zee after a nine year engagement.

Pinkerton's were soon on the trail of the gang, and between a confrontation with Cole and John, two detectives were left dead with Cole carrying his dead brother John home. The Pinkerton's, working on a tip, thought the James brothers would visit their mother at the Samuel's farm. On Jan. 26, 1875 when the sun set they surrounded the house and shouted for the brothers to surrender. Instead a light in the window went out, so the Pinkerton's threw a bomb through the window. There was a terrible cry and the attack left Mrs. Samuel without an arm and killed their mentally handicapped brother Archie. The newspapers picked up the story and shamed the detectives, "inexcusable and cowardly deed."

Jesse was outraged and over the course of his life planned and tried to fulfill several attempts at taking Allan Pinkerton's life while visiting Chicago. But according to Jesse the streets prevented him from what he suggested were a "dozen chances".

When money ran low, the brothers went back to work. Sometimes disagreeing to the point of holding a gun to one another. But cool heads prevailed, until the day of September 7, 1876, when in Minnesota, at the Northfield robbery only Jesse and Frank left without wounds. The wounded were captured and when asked why, Cole Younger said to the reporters, "We were drove to it." Likely referring to the battered southern economy and his war experience. The Northfield robbery made national news, and Jesse and Frank James celebrity criminals.

The following months they hid in dark quarters and ate only raw vegetables from farmhouses. They crept their way back slowly to Missouri. But even at home, they would not be publicly welcomed for the stories of innocent lives they affected. They took to a covered wagon into Tennessee bought two small farms near Nashville. Crime however, could not be stricken from their lives, and after another bloody robbery, the Missouri Governor Thomas T. Crittenden placed a $10,000 reward for the capture and conviction of Frank and Jesse James.

Jesse perhaps fearing very little and believing the dime novels made of him, was no longer hiding, but instead wore a thick black beard, and boasted with drama. "I'm Jesse James," he would say on his holdups, before introducing the rest of the gang as if were a show the victims were watching. The gang however, was no longer netting the same loot, much of it under $1,500.

Bob Ford, was the youngest of the Ford brothers who worked with Jesse. He also wasn't around for every heist. In reality he was teased and treated as more of an errand boy, which he resented.

Unbeknownst to Jesse, while the Ford brothers slept, they plotted his murder. Bob Ford had recently spoken to Governor Crittenden.

Jesse was planning his next robbery and asked the Ford brothers to come to his St. Joseph home. It was the morning of April 3, 1882 and his wife, Zee made breakfast, while their children played outside. After the meal, Jesse invited the Fords into the parlor to discuss how to rob the Platte County bank. Jesse had a newspaper at his hands with a headline about Dick Liddell's confession which referred to Bob Ford contacting the Governor. They began to act nervous as he glanced at it.

Jesse dropped the paper and stood up. He walked thoughtfully over to his window and watched outside at his children playing. Perhaps in a motion of reflecting on the importance of family, he noticed one of his family pictures hanging crooked. The Fords claim that Jesse took off his two gun belts, around his hips and shoulders, and looped it over the chair. (It was more likely, he was completely unarmed as he never wore guns in the house). The Fords continued, that Jesse took a stool and stepped up to fix the crooked frame. As his back was turned to the Fords, he apparently saw his fate through the glass. Bob lifted himself in a shaky disposition and at four feet shot several times to the back of his head. Jesse turned in horror but fell to the floor dead. Zee screamed and rushed to her husband, clinging and cradling him in her arms. Bob pretended it was an accident.

Every newspaper nationally mourned the infamous Jesse James, with headlines in memoriam, reading as the St. Joseph Gazette, "Goodbye, Jesse!"

Artist: Robert Karr

Frank James

Alexander Franklin James was born on January 10, 1843.

Frank partook in his actions cautiously and was less of a showman than his brother Jesse, and this ultimately led to his survival within the gang. While Frank often took a backstage to others in the gang, he was known to quote Shakespeare to brighten the mood.

On October 5, 1882, five months after his brother's murder, Frank felt it was time to give himself up. Frank walked into Governor Crittenden's office and placed his unbelted guns in front of him. "I want to hand over to you that which no living man except myself has been permitted to touch since 1861." The Governor promised Frank a fair trial for his surrender. National reporters gathered to the scene asking James a number of questions. "Why did you surrender? No one knew where you were hiding." Frank paused and said, "I was tired of an outlaw's life. I have been hunted for twenty-one years. I have literally lived in the saddle. I have never known a day of perfect peace. It was one long, anxious, inexorable, eternal vigil. When I slept it was literally in the midst of an arsenal. If I heard dogs bark more fiercely than usual, or the hooves of horses in a greater volume than usual, I stood to my arms. Have you an idea of what a man must endure who leads such a life? No, you cannot. No one can unless he lives it for himself."

His trial was set for August 21, 1883. A swarm of sympathy surrounded the case, measured with what the public saw as a cowardly act by Bob Ford, led to his acquittal. Frank returned to working on the Samuel's farm and later as a horse trainer. His experience and notoriety put him in a position also a racetrack starter. By the twentieth century, Frank was a commodity of the Old West and with his old friend Cole Younger, who had recently left prison, they took to the stage at a Wild West Show, sharing the spotlight. Frank died peacefully in his small bedroom at his farm on Feb. 18, 1915.

Henry Clay Vaughn

Henry "Hank" Clay Vaughn was born on April 27, 1849 to Alexander and Elizabeth Vaughn. The family lived on a farm in the Willamette River Valley of Oregon Territory (near present day Portland). Henry's paternal ancestry can be traced back to Trenewydd, Newton, Brecknockshire, Wales.

The Vaughn children numbered seven, and most of their time was spent time doing chores instead of schoolwork, this affected Henry's ability to write. The family also moved several more times in his youth, from The Dalles to Canyon City, Oregon. While in Canyon City, the Vaughn family looked to profit from the oncoming gold rush by supplying beef and horses to the miners.

Into his mid-teens, Henry was considered small at only 130 pounds. By this time though, he had already mastered a six-shooter and was deadly accurate. He was also becoming a heavy drinker. He was described as being finely dressed wearing a black frock coat, white shirt and black string tie. Vaughn's first run in was at the age of 15, when a William Headspot argued with Vaughn over non-payment of a horse. Headspot was killed and shortly after while Vaughn was still on bail he shot another man who filed the original complaint. Needless to say, he was taken to The Dulles jail for trial. The Vaughn family pleaded with the judge to allow Henry to change his life in the Army rather than face sentencing. The judge believed this could possible, but Henry lasted only 45 days before he was dishonorably discharged.

At 16, Henry became friends with a horse trader named Dan Burns and the two rode off to the gold fields of Idaho. In route, they stole a herd of horses in Umatilla County, Oregon which led to pursuit by Sheriff Frank Maddock and his deputy O.J. Hart. The law found Vaughn and Burns camping near Burnt River and approached quietly. It was in the morning, and the two were still apparently asleep, but when the blankets were ripped off the lawmen yelled for their arrest but Hart and Maddock were shot, and bullets were returned in a blaze. Burns and Hart laid dead while Maddock and Vaughn stumbled away with wounds. Vaughn fled on a horse, but was caught days later.

While in the Baker County Jail, Vaughn escaped the gallows again, and

Artist: Neale Howells

received a life sentence in Salem's territorial prison. Through a second family intervention, Vaughn left prison in February of 1870 pardoned by the Oregon governor. But while he was in prison he learned carpentry, bricklaying, black-smithing, and how to read and write.

Vaughn continued his work with horses and cattle, and built a shop in Toano, Nevada based on his new skills. His success led him to buy some land in Elko and marry to a Lois McCarty in May of 1875. Crime was not distant however, as Lois was a sister of the notorious McCarty brothers.

Vaughn and his wife had two children, both sons, named Alexander (1876) and Albert (1877). The boys were raised under difficult circumstances having their father absent most nights either gambling or drinking. While drunk, he was known to ride his horse into a saloon and shoot out lights or bottles off of bars. Lois had enough and left with their sons.

Moving to Arizona, Vaughn was in a gunfight and miraculously survived a bullet to the head. His errant ways led him back north to Pendleton, Oregon where he tried to slow down and sell horses and cattle again. On August 31, 1878 he married Louisa Jane Ditty. But rumors stirred he was dealing with Native Americans of the Umatilla Reservation who were rounding up strays from cattle drives in the Blue Mountains. Due to this, Vaughn setup a location in Spokane Falls, Washington, ideally sitting on a major cattle route to Montana. He continued his dealings taking any stray cattle along this pass for his own. He made his way back to Oregon, and there lived for a short time with his wife in a mountain cabin in Sturgill Basin. Louisa also left him.

Vaughn got wind of a vigilante committee forming to strike down cattle thieves. He made his way to Prineville, Oregon's Graham's Saloon where he found Charlie Long, a ranch boss who worked for the leader of the vigilante committee. The two commenced in a game of poker that quickly turned heated. The owner stopped it before it escalated but Long and Vaughn saw each other again in town at Til Glaze's Saloon. Vaughn tried to buy a round of drinks for everyone including Long, but Long refused and the two began to argue. Long reached for his gun and shot at Vaughn's head, grazing it slightly, while Vaughn returned with four pinpoint shots. Long was able to shot again striking Vaughn in the chest, but neither died that day.

Vaughn was tried at The Dalles, but as Long had fired the first shot he was acquitted. He left for Wood River, Idaho where he sold horses to the men working on a new railroad of the area. In town he met and married a widow named Martha Robie, who had a wealthy inheritance and owned land on the Umatilla Indian Reservation.

In a strange twist, Vaughn's wife often traveled by trains and in her presence it his work in foiling train robbers that he was awarded a lifetime pass for his good deeds.

Vaughn expanded his crooked business into Walla Walla and Spokane Falls, Washington, but times had changed and the railroad and fencing made it more difficult.

Although in a stable marriage, Vaughn never left his bad habits, and in 1886, he shot at Bill Falwell's feet to make him "dance." Falwell saw Vaughn the following day and shot him in the right arm. Later that year, Vaughn and his wife sold the farm and moved to Centerville, Washington.

On June 2, 1893, Vaughn arrived in Pendleton to get his horse shod, and while he waited he visited several bars. Apparently drunk and with his horse, he rode quickly up and down the Main Street with his horse yelling. But the horse slipped and shifted its weight on Vaughn crushing him from the fall. He suffered a skull fracture and died two weeks later on June 15, 1893 at 44 years. He was buried in this town at the Olney Cemetery in an unmarked grave.

Jesse Evans

Mystery surrounds the life of Jesse Evans, believed to be of Welsh descent, and according to one source part Cherokee. Evans was born in 1853 in Missouri. Early in his life he left his home and worked as a cowboy in Lampasas County, Texas. He moved again in 1872 to work at John Chisum's ranch, a decision that would put him shoulder to shoulder with petty criminals including Tom Hill, Frank Baker, and a teenager friend he met back in Silver City named Henry McCarty (later known as Billy the Kid). In his twenties, Evans was stealing cattle and committing armed robbery.

In September of 1877, Jesse Evans plotted with Hill, Baker, and a young Texan named Davis to steal cattle from Dick Brewer and John Tunstall's ranches. While Tunstall was away Brewer and his posse chased the thieves and exchanged a volley of shots. The four were arrested but escaped a few weeks later. Evans was wounded in a similar chase in January, 1878, within Grant County, New Mexico.

On Feb. 18, 1878, a posse was formed by Sheriff William Brady, including Evans, Hill and other Murphy-Dolan supporters. Evans and the posse approached Tunstall who was returning home from driving a herd of horses which were presently occupying his four men. Tunstall being alone, tried to negotiate with Evans and the posse, but Hill rode to the rear of Tunstall and cursed at him with a gunshot to the back of his head. Evans and the gang finished with several more shots before galloping away.

By December, Billy the Kid was looking to make peace with his old friend - Jesse Evans. At dusk, the two met in the middle of street and Evans said, "I ought to kill you right now," as several of his posse had been the victim of vigilante justice by the Kid. Jesse and McCarty spoke a few words and drew their guns aside and signaled to their men the fighting was over. The gangs celebrated that night and decided not to testify against each other in an upcoming trial.

Unfortunately for Evans, a young member of his gang named Billy Campbell was likely drunk, and was looking to prove himself, having not been around for the Lincoln County War. Campbell saw an unarmed local named Huston Chapman walk out of his house.

Artist: Jo Mazelis

Campbell pointed his pistol at the older man and yelled "Dance!" Chapman tried to remove the gun and was almost able to overtake Campbell when Dolan, standing behind him fired at him with Campbell releasing a shot from the front. Chapman mortally wounded fell to the ground. The two killers poured whiskey on the body and set him aflame. This would be the final straw for the territorial governor who looked to stamp out the crime in Lincoln. Evans, Dolan and Campbell were captured by the commander of Fort Stanton, while Billy the Kid escaped.

Billy the Kid knew his time was short and in an effort to receive amnesty from the governor gave his testimony against Evans, indicting the three. But Evans, Dolan and Campbell escaped the Fort Stanton jail on the night of March 19, 1879.

Evans moved out of state to Pecos County, Texas, where he continued his criminal habits. One particular gang robbery on July 3, 1880, led to a shootout with Texas Rangers near Presidio, Texas. Ranger George R. Bingham was gunned down and Evans was arrested.

On October 9th, Evans was convicted of murder in the second degree, and sentenced to ten years in the penitentiary for Bingham's death. He was just twenty seven at the time. Records describe him as being 5 feet 5 and ¾ inches, 150 pounds; with fair complexion, grey eyes, light hair; two large scars on his left thigh, and a bullet scar above and below his left elbow. The penitentiary leased Evans out to a contractor for road work. On May 23, 1882, he escaped a road gang, and vanished forever.

John Reynolds Hughes

John Reynolds Hughes was born February 11, 1855 in Henry County, Cambridge, Illinois. He was the son of Thomas Hughes and Jennie Bond. His grandparent had left Wales for America.

In 1865 the Hughes family relocated to Dixon and then later to Mound City, Kansas. By fourteen, John left home to work at a neighboring cattle ranch but soon headed west for Indian Territory. During his teens, he lived with Choctaw and Osage, and in one incident he was shot in the right arm during a scuffle. Through his time with them, he learned to track and hunt. He resettled amongst the Comanche in 1874, and worked in trade at Fort Sill, becoming friends with Quanah Parker. In his early twenties he worked as traildriver on the Chisholm Trail, and bought a farm near Liberty Hill, Travis County, Texas to sell beef and raise horses.

At this juncture of his life, Hughes enjoyed ranching but was unable to retract the slew of cattle thieves. In May 1886 he tracked a band of rustlers who had stolen horses from his and his neighbors' ranches. Several months later he found the men in northwestern Texas, killed four and sent the rest to New Mexico for arrest. The horses were returned to his neighbors and his heroism sparked an interest by the Texas Rangers.

By July 1887, Hughes sold his farm and was asked to partner with Texas Rangers to find an escaped murderer Judd Roberts. Roberts was tracked down and tried to resist arrest, being killed in the process. Hughes joined the Texas Rangers on August 10, 1887, and quickly went from Sergeant to Captain. Hughes border patrol service mostly focused on the area along the Rio Grande between Texas and Mexico.

Another notable feat came when Hughes was working undercover in a Shafter, Texas, silver mine where ore went missing. Hughes determined a foreman was the thief sending the missing silver on burro trains towards Mexico. He setup a trap at the mine and once the foreman was discovered a long shootout ensued with the Rangers being the victor.

Artist: Anthony Richards

In March 1896, Hughes was involved with the capture of notorious bandit Miguel de la Torre when they caught him on a street in Bajitas, Texas. Hughes held the position of captain and served as a ranger longer than any other person, retiring from the force in 1915. Zane Grey's story of the Long Ranger is even said to have been inspired by Hughes and his achievements.

Hughes, who was naturally quiet and reserved, never married, and possibly carried a form of post-traumatic stress which was not heard of then. But his work continued as chairman of the board of directors of the Citizens Industrial Bank of Austin. In 1940 he was the first to be awarded the Certificate of Valor, for the bravery of peace officers of the nation. After residing in El Paso, Hughes moved to Austin to spend the rest of his life with his niece, who looked after him. Hughes took his own life on June 3, 1947.

Major William H. Llewellyn

William Henry Harrison Llewellyn was born on September 9, 1851 in Monroe, Green County, Wisconsin. William's great-grandfather emigrated from Wales to Westmoreland County, Virginia.

After service in the Civil War, William's father moved his family to Iowa. William received a proper education in public school and later at Tabor College. At the age of fifteen, William left for Montana to strike it rich in the gold mining at Trinity Gulch. He left in 1874 without making a significant profit. He set his eyes on Omaha, Nebraska, where he speculated in land and briefly worked for the McCormick Reaper Company as a collector. Llewellyn married Ida May Little from Ohio, and with her they had seven children.

In 1877 Llewellyn was appointed a special agent in the Justice Department by President Hayes. His first assignment was at the Pine Ridge Indian Reservation where he was tasked with protecting the horses from rustling, specifically from the notorious Doc Middleton gang.

Llewellyn was transferred to the Mescalero Apache Reservation on June 16, 1881 in southern New Mexico. He worked as an Indian agent and quickly gained respect amongst some of the Apache. One of his roles was in forming an Indian police force and providing civil order. Llewllyn often hunted with them and was generally liked, giving him the name "Tata Crooked Nose." In two years he would also become the agent for the Jicarilla Apaches and led their movement to the Mescalero reservation. He later established an Indian boarding school, a doctor, and unified them into the Cattle Growers Association.

In the summer of 1885, Llewellyn resigned his government position as Indian agent when a Democrat candidate Grover Cleveland became President. Llewellyn moved to Las Cruces, and became partners with lawyers Rynerson and Wade, in southern New Mexico. From here, he served as a livestock agent for the Atchison, Topeka & Santa Fe Railroad Company.

In 1896 Llewellyn was involved with the Territorial House of Representatives and was chosen its speaker. He also took up many

Artist: Siobhan Owen

high profile cases including the Albert Jennings Fountain murder and disappearance.

At the start of the Spanish-American war in April 1898, the Governor of New Mexico called for a volunteer calvary force. Llewellyn helped in the recruiting process and led as Captain of one troop. His teenage son Morgan was in another troop under the command of future governor Captain George Curry. All together they were involved in the First U.S. Volunteer Cavalry.

The squadron left by train to San Antonio, Texas, and recruits could see a sign pointing the way: "Take This Car For The Exposition Grounds Where Roosevelt's Famous Rough Riders Are Camped". The name stuck and gained popularity. Training was in part with Lieutenant Colonel Theodore Roosevelt in command, and on May 29th, the troops were headed to Tampa, Florida. From Tampa they left for Cuba.

Captain Llewellyn showed great valor and was key in winning the hill (Kettle Hill) at San Juan. The story is told that a sentry was on night watch and heard Spanish troops approaching. The first person he told was Captain Llewellyn who helped raise the alarm for a counterattack in what was noted as Roosevelt's Rough Riders victory on San Juan Hill. Llewellyn's prompt action promoted him to Major and made him a war hero in La Cruces. Unfortunately, before he could go home Llewellyn succumbed to yellow fever and was hospitalized in New York City.

In 1901, Llewellyn was appointed United States attorney for New Mexico by newly elected President Roosevelt. His son, Morgan, was also given a title of surveyor general of the territory, a high ranking position akin to being governor. Both father and son left their posts on January 1, 1908 when they were involved with a scandal over land and mineral acquisitions by the Pennsylvania Development Company.

In the last decade, Llewellyn had been fighting for statehood of New Mexico, and by 1910 he was serving in the Constitutional Convention and in 1911 as a member of New Mexico's first state legislature. On June 11, 1927, Llewellyn died in the U.S. Army William Beaumont hospital in El Paso.

Artist: Nichola Hope

John T. Morris

Sheriff John Thomas Morris, of Welsh descent, was born October 30, 1853, to N.N. and Ann Morris. Morris notably shot down outlaw Jim C. Reed the husband of Belle Starr on August 6, 1874. Reed with two others had held up the San Antonio and Austin stagecoach on the 7th of April. A reward of "Dead or Alive" was soon placed on the robbers heads not exceeding three thousand dollars. John T. Morris, a citizen of Collin County, in his duties as Deputy Sheriff pursued the stage robbers.

On October 25, 1894, Morris was commissioned a deputy out of Ft. Smith, Arkansas, and listed his place of residence as Edna, Kansas. It is believed that Morris was once a member of the Jim Reed Gang and a distant relative, third or fourth cousin. Thus, he was on friendly terms and able to gain the trust of Reed. Reed was a known gunslinger having rode with the Quantrill's Raiders and while in Carthridge, Missouri, Reed fell in love with Belle Shirley, a lady who would become the "Queen of the Outlaws". Reed took Belle against her father's wishes to Texas where they raised a son, Ed, and a daughter, Pearl Younger, who was born to outlaw Cole Younger.

On August 6, 1875, Reed's final moments were told by a cousin named William,

"Jim and a man named John T. Morris were riding along the road, horseback. They came to a farmhouse and decided to go in and get the woman to cook up something. Morris said that sight of their guns would make the woman nervous and suggested they leave them on their saddles, which was done. After the two had eaten, Morris said he had swallowed a fly and would have to go out and relieve himself. He hurried to the horses, retrieved his pistol, slipped it into his pocket, and came back where Jim was sitting. Suddenly he whipped out his six-shooter and said, 'Jim, I'm arresting you on the charge of robbery. Now don't make me any trouble.' Jim leaped up, seized the table and rushed upon Morris. Morris seized the table and the two wrestled all over the room, grunting and cursing, they lady of the house screaming, making, in all, quite a fracas. Jim began pummelin' Morris in the face with his fist. Morris shot through the table and hit Jim in the stomach. In a few minutes Jim was dead. Morris's face was pulpy, for Jim had given him some lusty blows."

Reed's body was taken to McKinney, Texas for identification and burial. One source in Harman in Hell on the Border claims Belle Starr was there to identify Reed but said to Morris 'you will have to kill Jim Reed if you wish to secure the reward'.

Morris was given one thousand dollars by the state for his actions, and after collecting the bounty he purchased a farm near Bowie, Texas. He settled down and showed his gentler side in growing ornamental flowers. On occasion, the United States Marshall would bring him back to service in an effort to keep Sooners out of Oklahoma Territory. Even in later life, he carried the nickname "Lightning Jack" for his gun slinging.

A descendant of Morris reveals his grandfather's past was kept mostly private, but in his final years he went with his son to shoot at targets. After successfully shooting tin cans, he handed his pistol to his son and said go ahead and try it. His son, was a school teacher, and aimed at his target but missed. "The way of the gun is dead," Morris said taking the pistol back in his hand, "and it's for the best."Morris died March 27, 1934 and was buried in Green Hill Cemetery, McClain County, Oklahoma.

William R. "Jake" Owen

Owen was reportedly born in Wales on May 27, 1857. He was raised in Cape Girardeau, Missouri and relocated with his parents to Uvalde, Texas when he was seventeen. In 1876, he left his home and joined a cattle drive to Arizona. He helped drive Robert K. Wylie's herd of 8,000 cattle from Texas to New Mexico with riders Sam Coggin and Clay Parks. After the drive, he begun work Robert K. Wylie on a regular basis. Around 1878, Owen fought on the side of the Dolan Faction during the Lincoln County War. In 1933 he gave testimony about the events.

He stayed in New Mexico for the remainder of his days, working with his own herd of cattle and for Clay Allison of the Hash Knife Cattle Company. Later in life he worked with Milo Pierce, and the two built a rock house that would be sold to Clay Allison.

Between 1895 and 1908, Owen served as the second county clerk for Carlsbad. He married and had one daughter. On December 24, 1939, Owen died in Carlsbad, New Mexico.

John Wightman (Frank Clifford)

John Wightman was born in Panteg, near the mining town of Pontypool, Wales on March 18, 1860 to James Temple Wightman and Sarah Walker.

Wightman speaks of his home, "The Wern," as it was known, "was located in Monmouthshire. When I was eleven years of age, my father brought me across the ocean and out to New Mexico. I remember crossing Kansas in a train, and seeing my first herd of buffalo through the train windows…It was a marvelous sight to a young boy to see that great herd of shaggy beasts, several miles wide and reaching all the way back to the horizon, coming along in waves the way they do-wave after wave like the waves of the ocean."

At the age of 11, his family moved to Cimarron, New Mexico Territory, where his father worked for the Maxwell Land Grant and Railroad Company. "We took the stage over the Raton Pass, and eventually we arrived in Cimarron. There my father had a very high position with the Maxwell Land Grant and Railway Company." When his father died in 1874, Wightman took to ranch work, and thoroughly enjoyed it. Here he met and befriended outlaw Clay Allison and as he wrote in his memoirs, "rode with him in some of the stirring incidents of the Colfax County war."

Clay Allison arrived in Colfax County around 1870 when the fall of the Maxwell Land Grant and Railway Company left cowmen and settlers fighting a political ring over the land claims, provoking vigilante justice. Allison called his ruffians the "Law and Order League" of which Wightman was a part. The group rode off the oppressive political ring that was part of the old grant company and destroyed its affiliate "Cimarron News and Press".

In the summer of 1875, a reverend named Franklin Tolby exposed the corruption of the political ring in power. He had to report this in a St. Louis paper as the local press of Cimarron was a puppet of the ring. Tolby was murdered and found hidden in the brush near Elizabethtown where he preached on September 14. Two Mexican men were suspected, and one confessed of being paid by the ring for the job. While the one that confessed was hanged, the other who kept things secret was sent to be kept in protective custody by the ring's ally Sheriff

Artist: Rhys Jones

Rhinehart in the Cimarron jail. However, Allison got word and called the "Law and Order League" together and set out to the jailhouse, where he seized an opportunity to get revenge, Allison with three of his men waited for the arrival of the sheriff and the murderer. Rhinehart and a deputy was seen taking the murderer to jail, with both of his hands tied between them. Allison stepped out first and said, "Just a minute," to which they turned to face the gang. Allison fired at the murderer and quickly said, "That's all, boys!" As they took horseback and rode off in celebration.

After several incidents, the government put Colfax County under martial law, sending all those involved to Taos for trial. Seeing how each man was still wearing their holster, they were released as quickly they were tried. By 1880, Wightman was with Charlie Siringo in New Mexico trying to recover some of the cattle stolen by Billy the Kid and his cohorts. Wightman led a mysterious life under several pseudonyms including Frank Wightman and Frank Clifford. He also was given the nickname "Big Foot Wallace".

Menham eventually settled in Emporia, Kansas, where he went under the radar with the name of John Francis Wallace. Here he found work on the railroad and married Sarah Frances Timmons with whom they had seven children.

By 1940, the eighty one year old Menham met a portrait painter named Mrs. Frickel on board a train near Wichita, Kansas. For the first time in forty years, Menham spoke of his adventures as she painted his portrait. The portrait would go on to win her first prize in a Wichita contest, while with the help of Frickel, Menham published his stories in the book Deep Trails in the Old West: A Frontier Memoir under the pseudonym Frank Clifford.

Menham died on September 8, 1946 in North Little Rock, Pulaski, Arkansas.

David Robert Evans

David Robert Evans was born in Aberystwyth, Wales on March of 1862 and was raised in Towyn. He and his brother first traveled to the United States in the 1880s, while his brother went home, David chose to stay settling in Minnesela, Dakota Territory.

David married Nellie Pratt who died in childbirth. He remarried around 1900 to Myrtle Viola White from Illinois. They had a daughter named Lelia who married Wilbur Peugh (designer of the Cow Palace in San Francisco).

Evans was a cowboy, rancher, bank cashier and President of the First National Bank of Belle Fourche, South Dakota. In 1917 he also served as South Dakota State Senator.

By 1918, Evans and other community leaders promoted a rodeo in Belle Fourche to raise money for World War I. While the total population of the town was only 1,410, their attendance reached over 15,000, making it a huge success. The Roundup is now one of the oldest continuously held outdoor rodeos in America. Evans served as their President in 1927.

During the winter of 1928, Evans close friend Peter Thompson died in a sanatorium. He wrote of Thompson's forgotten service in the Battle of the Little Big Horn (a Congressional Medal of Honor recipient). Many believed no soldier survived, but it was Thompson's account that gave the soldier's perspective, as he was shot carrying water and caring for the dying troops, against his officer's command.

In 1929, Evans helped found the Rodeo Association of America which looked to standardize the event in establishing a point system, and determine a champion cowboy.

On February 14, 1939 Evans died and was buried in Pine Slope Cemetery, Belle Fourche.

Artist: Jo Mazelis

Robert Mills (Owen Roscomyl)

Born Robert Scourfield Mills, Jr. in Southport, Merseyside on September 6, 1863 to parents Robert Sr. and Jane Ann Scowfield. The family moved to Lancashire where he was raised, and as a child, Mills Jr. was highly influenced by his maternal grandmother, who was born in Tremeirchion in North Wales.

At fifteen Mills left his home and traveled to America. Living as a cowboy in Colorado, Wyoming, Montana and California. He also worked in the mining camps his wrote fanciful stories of his adventures. In January of 1881 he wrote from Wyoming Territory:

One day, as I was riding back to camp, a fellow rode out in front of me with a revolver in his hand; he held it close to my nose telling me to throw up my hands. I was wearing the grizzly skin for a cloak and had concealed my right arm in it. I threw up my left arm telling him I had but one. 'That so,' said he, lowering his pistol. 'Wal, I want yer hoss, savvy to the racket?' 'Yes,' I said, 'heap good savvy,' and like lightning I put my pistol between his eyes, and told him to drop his pistol and jump off his horse which he did. I caught his horse with my left hand, keeping the road agent covered with my pistol in my right and, digging spurs into my horse, was gone followed by half a dozen bullets from the road agent's pistol.

Upon returning to England he served in the 1st Royal Dragoons between 1887 and 1890. He was involved in the Boer War as a captain of Howard's Canadian Scouts. In 1902 he arrived back in Wales and began promoting Welsh culture from organizing the National Pageant of Wales in 1909 to writing books on the Prince of Wales in 1911. He became a proficient author of several novels including *Old Fireproof* and topics of Welsh history, notably *Flame-bearers of Welsh history*. His pen-names being Owen Rhoscomyl and Owen Vaughan.

In December of 1901, Mills married Catherine Geere, who he met in South Africa, and to whom they had four children: Rhys, Olwen, Nest and Emrys Llewellyn. Mills died October 15, 1919. Mills was buried in Rhyl Cemetery in Denbighshire, Wales.

Artist: Kerry Evans

John Perrett (Potato Creek Johnny)

John E. Perrett (or Parrott) was born in Wales between 1866 and 1873. Perrett emigrated with his mother Mary A. Perrett to the United States around 1883 or 1884, and he was estimated to be around twelve or thirteen at the time. It is unknown what became of his father or what occurred for this change. Perrett attended school in Lawrence, South Dakota, where he is listed in a school enrollment of 1887 at the age of 14. John Bell was listed as his guardian during these years. Bell was a noted rancher of the area having originally come from Yorkshire, England. He married a woman by the name of Mary on January 20, 1872 in Pittsburgh, Pennsylvania. Bell seeking wealth in mining left with his family to the Dakota Territory where John Perrett's early years were spent as a cowhand with his seven step-siblings. Bell later worked as a postmaster of Spearfish. Into adulthood, Perrett followed an Episcopal religious view and married in 1911 (another source has March 13, 1907) to Molley Hamilton of Belle Fourche. Apparently they had at least two children of their own Jesse and Eva. Perrett began working a claim on Potato Creek, an offshoot of Spearfish Creek. His appearance changed to that of a typical prospector, long hair and beard earning him the nickname "Potato Creek Johnny." He and his wife struggled financially for decades, divorcing in 1928.

In the following year, Perrett found what he called his "leg-shaped" gold nugget, the largest historical find to date. Some historians suggest that the nugget was actually several melted gold pieces together. Whatever it was, it changed his luck. By 1931, Perrett was considered a veteran miner and respected member of the community. He was now working with others to extract more. Perrett sold the nugget for $250 to the Adams Museum. His notoriety increased immediately, making the nugget and Perrett a tourist attraction. Visitors would want to see the miner in action, and he would entertain them in his cabins with fanciful stories as he worked. If a person asked about the nugget, he'd routinely say, "I have been looking for the rest of the leg ever since". Perrett was a major attraction for Deadwood, helping host events and being involved in the local parades.

Perrett died on February 26, 1943 and was buried at the Mt. Moriah Cemetery with notable townsfolk Calamity Jane, Wild Bill Hickok, and Seth Bullock.

Willa Cather

Wilella Sibert Cather was born December 7, 1873 in the Black Creek Valley of Virginia to parents Charles Fectigue Cather and Mary Virginia Boak. Cather's family originated in Wales, the family name deriving from Cadair Idris, a mountain range in northwestern Wales.

Cather grew up on her family farm (Willowshade) in Virginia, and was home schooled. She enjoyed her freedom outdoors, but in 1883 the farm was sold and the family moved west to the Nebraskan frontier. Soon after, they left the rugged conditions for a slightly gentler life in Red Cloud, where her father worked in banking.

While in Nebraska, Cather went to public school and later attended the University of Nebraska in 1891. As a student she published her stories and this she choose as her career by her graduation in 1896.

She first took work as a manager and editor at the Pittsburgh Home Monthly, followed by a position as copy editor and cultural reviewer at the Pittsburgh Daily Ledger. In 1901, she worked as a teacher and friended Isabelle McClung, a wealthy art patron, who offered her a home to write.

During this productive time, she wrote April Twilight, a book of poems, in 1903, and in 1905 the Troll Garden, a book of tales. C.S. McClure became a fan and invited her to join his staff of McClure's magazine. Cather quickly elevated to managing editor by 1908.

Through a friend's suggestion, Cather went full time as a fiction writer. In 1913 she published *O Pioneers!* to a strong reception and in 1918 My Antonia. Both tell the stories of pioneer women on the Nebraskan Great Plains. The Song of the Lark was published in 1915 and her Pulitzer Prize-winning novel, One of Ours, was published in 1922. The novel revolves around the life of a man's journey from Nebraska to his death in World War I.

Cather received acclimation by many institutions including Yale, New York University, and Smith College. She was also elected to the National Institute of Arts and Letters. On April 24, 1947, Cather died in New York City.

Artist: Penny Richards

Artist: Xavier Lopez Jr.

Harvey Alexander Logan (Kid Curry)

Sources conflict about his birth date being either 1865 or 1867 in Tama, Iowa. Logan and his younger brothers were orphans and taken in to live with their aunt, Mrs. Hiram Lee, in Dodson, Missouri. The Logan children were of Scottish and Welsh descent through emigrants of Lewis and Flemish Counties in Kentucky.

Logan and his brothers befriended a man named "Flat Nose" George Curry who may have been a mentor of sorts to the boys as they soon took his last name of "Curry".

When Logan was in his late teens he rode with a cattle drive to Pueblo, Colorado with his brothers and cousin Bob Lee. He got into an altercation at a saloon and the boys skipped town towards southern Wyoming.

The next year they homesteaded on a horse ranch in Chouteau County, Montana just south of the Landusky Mining Camp. They became rustlers and in 1888 they had stolen enough to start their own ranch on the property.

On October 2, 1894, Logan and his brother Johnnie and brother-in-law, Lee Self, fought with a neighbor named James Ross. Logan would be arrested for assault with a deadly weapon.

Logan had an evil temper and when drunk was deadly. In 1894, he feuded with Powell "Pike" Landusky, a miner and founder of a town that bared his name. Landusky claimed Logan was romantic with his daughter. When in fact it was secretly Johnnie who was the father of her baby. Logan pummeled Landusky and went to jail. He was released shortly after on grounds of self-defense. But Logan ran into Landusky again while drinking in a saloon and the two went at it. Landusky pulled a gun and threatened the unarmed Logan. His brothers threw him a pistol while Landusky fired but the pistol jammed. Logan slowly raised his gun and shot him in the head.

Logan fled to New Mexico knowing he would not receive a fair trial. In late 1895, Logan began riding with Thomas Ketchum's Black Jack gang.

In January of 1896, Logan heard a friend of Landusky named James Winter was bragging he would collect the reward on his head. Logan returned to Montana with his brothers to pay him a visit at his ranch. The forthcoming shootout was disastrous leaving Johnnie dead. Logan plotted revenge and heand his remaining brother Lonnie escaped back to New Mexico to Black Jack Ketchum's gang.

In a disagreement over money earned in a train robbery, Logan and his brother left the gang and headed north to Colorado working on a ranch near Sand Gulch.

This time Logan started his own gang with brother, Lonnie, Walt Putman, Tom O'Day and George Curry. In April of 1897, the gang was rustling horses and Logan killed a chasing Deputy Sheriff William Deane of Powder River, Wyoming.

Logan was captured that year in Belle Fourche, South Dakota when he was shot through the wrist. The gang spent time in Deadwood, South Dakota but managed to escape on October 31, 1897.

On July 14, 1898, Logan joined Sundance Kid and George Curry in a train heist but little was collected. In the following year, on June 2, the Wild Bunch took over a Union Pacific Railroad near Wilcox, Wyoming. In the chase Sheriff Joe Hazen was killed and the gang hid out in the Hole-in-the-Wall on the Colorado/Utah border. At this point, Pinkerton agents were called into service.

Logan went to New Mexico with Butch Cassidy and on July 11, 1899, they robbed a train near Folsom, New Mexico, resulting in the death of Sheriff Ed Farr and his deputy Henry Love and gang member Sam Ketchum. Logan made his way to San Antonio, where he lived in Fannie Porter's Brothel. Here he met and had a long term relationship with Della Moore aka Annie Rogers.

In 1900 lawmen killed both Lonnie and George Curry in separate circumstances. In March, Logan and Will Carver were found in St. Johns, Arizona, trying to pass stolen notes. This led to three more lawmen being killed in pursuit. Escaping to the WS Ranch in Alma, New Mexico where Butch Cassidy and Elza Lay worked, Logan and Carver shook off two more lawmen, killing another.

On May 26, Logan rode to Moab, Utah to settle the score for George Curry's death, taking the life of Grand County Sheriff John Tyler and his deputy, Sam Jenkins. Logan was again with Wild Bunch when it robbed a train on August 29, 1900, near Tipton, Wyoming, profiting $55,000. Logan was by now seen as the "tiger of the Wild Bunch" and the "Wildest of the Wild Bunch". The group continued to steal from trains and banks and hid out in the Hole-in-the-Wall country. Another major robbery occurred near Wagner, Montana on July 3, 1901 making off with an estimated $40,000.

By this time, Logan had killed sheriffs in Wyoming, Utah, and Arizona. He also killed Jim Winters out of revenge of his brother. Being one of the most wanted men in the country, Logan hid in Knoxville, Tennessee. His ways did not stop though, having announced himself again after a shootout with the law. He struck three policemen but was also shot in the shoulder. Bleeding prefusely he fled but was captured thirty miles away. In his trial he was scheduled to be sent to a maximum security prison in Columbus, Ohio. But along the trip he made a daring escape from the Knoxville jail. Logan tied several pieces of cloth together and wire from a broom to hook and pully a guard close to the cell. Successfully he took his keys and stole his pistols. Out the door he used another guard as a shield Using a second guard as a human shield, he ordered the guard to saddle the sheriff's horse. In doing so, he rode out of town to freedom.

Pinkerton's were calling Kid Curry the most dangerous outlaw in America, and his track record seemed to prove it. But having recently taken a group photo of the gang, he was now a prime target.

Butch Cassidy and the Sundance Kid had also evaded capture when they relocated operations in Argentina. Logan tried to join them but was unable to do so and instead hid out in Colorado. In June of 1904, he rallied a gang of his own but after a botched train robbery he was chased down and was either shot or committed suicide near Parachute, Colorado.

Rumors even suggest he lived and made his way to Argentina where he survived in his dealings until 1910 or 1911 when he was killed.

Old West ghost towns that have Welsh origins

Ajax, Utah
Welsh immigrant William Ajax started a department store in the Rush Valley area of southeastern Tooele County, Utah. The success of the store sparked interest in building a town around it. Popularity of the Ajax Underground Store lasted until the owner's death in 1899 when residents left the following year.

Lissie, Texas
Many Welsh miners came to live here during an economic downturn in Great Britain starting in 1876. The Workmen's Emigration Society was established in 1878 to move these families to Texas.

Nevadaville, Colorado
Welsh miners worked the gold mining town in Gilpin County and left a distinctive mark in the stonework.

Nortonville, California
A once coal mining town with a dense population of Welsh emigrants.

Padonia, Kansas
David Evans, a Welsh farmer founded the township of Padonia with ten families all of which came from Wales.

Penryn, California
In 1864 Penryn was founded by a Welsh immigrant named Griffith Griffith when he helped build a granite quarry on lease from the Central Pacific Railroad. Griffith gave it this name for his home in North Wales, where his father worked in the Penrhyn Slate Quarry. The word penrhyn translates in Welsh to headland or promontory, in corrolation to the seaport.

Spring Canyon, Utah
In many mining ghost towns residents tell a story of a ghost known in part as the White Lady. In Spring Canyon, this story lingers and speaks of Welsh miners who were superstitious of women in the coal mines. It was said that any woman who went near the mine might bring unintential disaster. This superstition is thought to go back to the first coal mines in Wales when women helped in hualing coal in baskets.

They strapped the baskets around their heads crawling carefully on their hands and knees. However, there is also a Welsh story of the Gwyllion, a frightful female fairy or banshee, who resides in the mountains and leads naive men to their demise. The Gwyllion is said to dress in a beautiful white dress floating near the mining camp. Her presence was attractive at glance as she lured the men into the mine. Following her meant sure disaster.

As the author I must share my own real experience upon visiting Calico ghost town in Yerma, California. I was in the town after hours during their Calico Days festival. It was around seven at night and pitch black except for the stars. I was heading towards the parking lot with my family having just left where a few people in western period clothing were camping in town. Thus it would not be strange to see a woman wandering about in an old dress, but as my family stopped to look at the stars, I saw a lady in a fancy white dress approach. Her dress was all I could see of her. I could not see her face, nor heard her footsteps. Being a little uncomfortable with her I said "Evening." But she didn't respond. She passed at a distance of about five feet. I was distracted again by my family and we walked further thinking nothing more of it. Then, there was now another family at about twelve feet from us and I could again see the lady in white now circling back towards the town at the opposite side of the lot, with the other family between us seemingly unaware of her. I decided to point her out this time to my family as her white form was hazy and jokingly said, "look at the ghost." They both acknowledged her and thought her strange and we all watched her fade into the darkness. It was not until I was asleep and awoke in the middle of the night I realized what I had witnessed floating by me earlier that evening. I told my wife and she also claimed to not see her until I pointed her out. When I asked a historian on site the following day they confirmed I had seen the White Lady.

Swansea, California
Many Welsh miners emigrated from Swansea in south Wales to work this now desolate mining area.

Wales, Utah
Welsh followers of Brigham Young settled here in 1854 to mine the "rock that burns".

References

1787 The Adventures of Col. Daniel Boon, Formerly a Hunter: Containing a Narrative of the Wars of Kentucky. The American Magazine.

1836 Evelyn Brogan. James Bowie: A Hero of the Alamo. Theodore Kunzman Printer & Publisher.

1874 Austin Weekly Democratic Statesman August 9.

1874 Dallas Daily Herald August 28, 1874

1874 Galveston Daily News August 9, 1874

1898. The laws of Texas 1822-1897, Texas, Coahuila and Texas (Mexico), Coahuila and Texas (Mexico). The Gammel Book Company

1900 Robert Vaughn. Then and Now: Or, Thirty-six Years in the Rockies. Personal Reminiscences of Some of the First Pioneers of the State of Montana. Indians and Indian Wars. The Past and Present of the Rocky Mountain Country. 1864-1900. Tribune Printing Company.

1904 Doane Robinson. History of South Dakota, Vol. II

1909: 304, Matt Bushnell Jones, History of the Town of Waitsfield, Vermont, 1782-1908: With Family Genealogies, G. E. Littlefield)

1912 Ralph Emerson Twitchell. The Leading Facts of New Mexico History Vol. II. The Torch Press.

1931 Mrs. Annie Anderson. New York Evening Post. Friday, April 10, 1931.

1931 Pioneer Dies. The Niagara Falls Gazette. Friday, April 10, 1931.

1931 Woman Who Knew Says Men of West Weren't So Brave. The Southeast Missourian, April 17, 1931.

1953 Richard Cleghorn Overton. Gulf to Rockies: The Heritage of the

Fort Worth and Denver, Colorado and Southern Railways. University of Texas Press.

1955 Ed Ellsworth Bartholomew. Jesse Evans, a Texas Hide-burner. Frontier Press of Texas.

1958 George Curry. George Curry 1861-1947 An Autobiography. Univ. of New Mexico Press.

1961 Mildred R. Bennett. The World of Willa Cather. University of Nebraska Press.

1962. John Clay. My Life on the Range. Norman: University of Oklahoma Press.

1962 Alpheus Hoyt Favour. Old Bill Williams, Mountain Man. University of Oklahoma Press.

1962 William Keleher. The Fabulous Frontier. Univ. of New Mexico Press.

1968 Larson, Robert Larson. George Curry. New Mexico Historical Review XLIII:4.

1969 Elsie V. Hanauer. The Old West: People and Places. A.S. Barnes and Company.

1971. John R. Burroughs, Guardian of the Grasslands. Cheyenne: Pioneer Printing Stationery Co.

1971 Vernon Gladden Spence. Colonel Morgan Jones. University of Oklahoma Press.

1973 C.L. Sonnichsen. The Mescalero Apaches. Univ. of Oklahoma Press.

1979 William S. Powell, editor. Dictionary of North Carolina Biography, 6 volumes. University of North Carolina Press.

1981 W. Raymond Wood. The John Evans 1796-97 Map of the Missouri River. Great Plains Quarterly. Paper 1920. University of Missouri-Columbia.

1982 LeRoy Reuben Hafen. Mountain Men and Fur Traders of the Far West: Eighteen Biographical Sketches. University of Nebraska Press.

1982 Winona Morris Nation. Author Does Justice to Famous Woman Outlaw. Edmond Evening News, Thursday, Sept. 16, 1982

1985 Virgil E. Baugh. Rendezvous at the Alamo: Highlights in the Lives of Bowie, Crockett, and Travis. University of Nebraska Press.

1987 Ronald D. Dennis. Dan Jones, Welshman: Taking the Gospel Home. The Church of Jesus Christ of Latter-Day Saints.

1988 Paul Iselin Wellman. The Trampling Herd: The Story of the Cattle Range in America. University of Nebraska Press.

1991 Bill O'Neal. Encyclopedia of Western Gunfighters. University of Oklahoma Press.

1991 Dan L. Thrapp. Encyclopedia of Frontier Biography. University of Nebraska Press.

1991 Lawrence M. Woods. Wyoming Biographies. Worland WY: High Plains Publishing Co.

1992 Jay Robert Nash. Encyclopedia of Western Lawmen & Outlaws. Paragon House.

1995 Paxton P. Price. Pioneers of the Mesilla Valley. Yucca Tree Press.

2003 J.R. Edmondson. Jim Bowie: Frontier Legend, Alamo Hero. The Rosen Publishing Group.

2003 James Hervey Simpson. Navajo Expedition: Journal of a Military Reconnaisance from Santa Fe, New Mexico to the Navaho Country Made in 1849. University of Oklahoma Press.

2004 David J. Wishart. Encyclopedia of the Great Plains. University of Nebraska Press.

2006 Linda S. Watts. Encyclopedia of American Folklore. Infobase Publishing.

2007 Ralph Emerson Twitchell. The Leading Facts of New Mexican History, Volume II. Sunstone Press.

2007 William A. Keleher. Violence in Lincoln County, 1869-1881. Sunstone Press.

2008 C.R. Caldwell. Dead Right: The Lincoln County War.
2009 Erin H. Turner. Badasses of the Old West: True Stories of Outlaws on the Edge. Rowman & Littlefield.

2009 Kathryn Cullen-DuPont. Encyclopedia of Women's History in America. Infobase Publishing.

2012 Frank Clifford. Deep Trails in the Old West: A Frontier Memoir. University of Oklahoma Press.

2013 Robert Hunter. Notes on David Roberts Evan. Washington, DC

2014 Robert Vaughn. Then and Now: Thirty-Six Years in the Rockies, 1864-1900. Farcounty Press.

2015 Ian Shine. Thomas Hunt Morgan: Pioneer of Genetics. University Press of Kentucky.

http://www.civilwar.org/education/history/biographies/john-hunt-morgan-1.html

Scanned at http://files.usgwarchives.net/sd/biography/doane2/bell.txt

South Dakota, School Records, 1879-1970
South Dakota, State Census, 1915
South Dakota, State Census, 1925
Texas, Deaths, 1890-1976 Vol 055, certificates 027

The Contributors:

Lorin Morgan-Richards was born in 1975 in Beebetown, Ohio. Richards is an author, poet and illustrator. Richards graduated with a BA in Cultural Anthropology from California State University, Los Angeles. Richards is owner of A Raven Above Press, Publisher and Editor-in-chief of Celtic Family Magazine and was the co-founder and Executive Director of the Los Angeles St. David's Day Festival. Richards serves as Director Emeritus with the Welsh League of Southern California. Richards ancestor was the second generation Welsh American poet Robert Dennison Morgan.

www.lorinrichards.com

Jude Johnson has been a history enthusiast since childhood and has spoken about her historical research at numerous historical societies as well as BBC Radio Wales. She loves the smell of old parchment and has been known to become lost for hours among the maps and old photographs in numerous historical societies. She is a member of Gecko Gals Ink, LLC, a group of "sassy Tucson authors" who encourage other writers to become published by holding writing seminars and classes. While she has no Welsh heritage, Jude has actively studied Cymraeg—the Welsh Language and Welsh history.

www.jude-johnson.com

Special thanks to Valerie, Karen, Robert Conrad, the National Welsh American Foundation, the Welsh League of Southern California, and all the artists involved (mentioned in no particular order): Anna Hughes, Michele Witchipoo, Nichola Hope, Siobhan Owen, Kimberly Wlassak, Carys Evans, Sarah Hope, Briana Lopez, Shelby Criswell, Karen M. Richards, Geri E. Gallas, Siobhan Owen, Rochelle Rosenkild, Jo Mazelis, Robert Karr, Neale Howells, Anthony Richards, Rhys Jones, Kerry Evans, Penny Richards, and Xavier Lopez Jr.

www.aravenabovepress.com

www.ingramcontent.com/pod-product-compliance
Lightning Source LLC
Chambersburg PA
CBHW050604300426
44112CB00013B/2059